THE HUTCHINSON
BOOK OF POST-WAR
BRITISH POETS

BY THE SAME AUTHOR

Poetry

Walking Under Water
Tenants of the House
Poems, Golders Green
A Small Desperation
Funland and Other Poems
Collected Poems 1948–1976
Way Out in the Centre
Ask the Bloody Horse
White Coat, Purple Coat

Plays

House of Cowards
The Dogs of Pavlov
Pythagoras (Smith)

Novels

Ash on a Young Man's Sleeve
Some Corner of an English Field
O Jones, O Jones

Other Prose

A Poet in the Family (Autobiography)
A Strong Dose of Myself (Confessions, Stories, Essays)
Journals from the Ant-Heap

THE HUTCHINSON BOOK OF POST-WAR BRITISH POETS

SELECTED BY DANNIE ABSE

Hutchinson
London Sydney Auckland Johannesburg

This edition first published in Great Britain by Hutchinson,
an imprint of Century Hutchinson Ltd, Brookmount House,
62–65 Chandos Place, London WC2N 4NW

Century Hutchinson Australia (Pty) Ltd
20 Alfred Street, Milsons Point, Sydney, NSW 2061 Australia

Century Hutchinson New Zealand Limited
PO Box 40-086, Glenfield, Auckland 10, New Zealand

Century Hutchinson South Africa (Pty) Ltd
PO Box 337 Berglvei, 2012 South Africa

British Library Cataloguing in Publication Data
The Hutchinson book of post-war British poets

   I. Abse. Dannie, 1923–
821'.914'08

ISBN 0091737966

Printed and bound in Great Britain by
Courier International Ltd, Tiptree, Essex

While every effort has been made to trace copyright,
the publisher would like to apologize to anyone who
has not been formally acknowledged.

CONTENTS

Fleur Adcock 1934–
For a Five-year-old
Leaving the Tate
Future Work
The Bullaun

Patricia Beer 1924–
The Faithful Wife
The Letter

James Berry 1924–
Lucy's Letter

Thomas Blackburn 1916–1977
Teaching Wordsworth
Francis Bacon
Laudanum

Alison Brackenbury 1953–
Gallop

Edwin Brock 1927–
Song of the Battery Hen

George Mackay Brown 1921–
Ikey on the People of Hellya
Love Letter

Alan Brownjohn 1931–
Office Party
Formosavej
In a Restaurant

Michael Burn 1912–
In Japan

John Cassidy 1928–
An Attitude of Mind
Frozen Canal
Disturbance

Charles Causley 1917–
Ou Phrontis
Family Feeling
Timothy Winters

Gillian Clarke 1937–
The Hare
Overheard in County Sligo

Stewart Conn 1936–
Farm Funeral
Visiting Hour

Tony Conran 1931–
Elegy for the Welsh
Dead, in the Falkland Islands,
1982

David Constantine 1944–
Watching for Dolphins

Wendy Cope 1945–
Engineers' Corner

Kevin Crossley-Holland
Dusk, Burnham-Overy-
Staithe

Tony Curtis 1946–
The Freezer
Summer in Greece

Donald Davie 1922–
Cherry Ripe
The Fountain
Put Not Your Trust in Princes

Carol Ann Duffy 1955–
Standing Female Nude
The Virgin Punishing the
Infant

Douglas Dunn 1942–
The Patricians
The Friendship of Young
Poets
Leaving Dundee
A Snow-walk

D. J. Enright 1920–
Jingle Bells
Master Kung at the Keyboard
Seaside Sensation
Abbey Going

Ruth Fainlight 1931–
Animal Tamer
Introspection of a Sibyl

U. A. Fanthorpe 1929–
Not My Best Side
Rising Damp
'Soothing and Awful'

Elaine Feinstein 1930–
Anniversary
Mother Love

James Fenton 1949–
In a Notebook

Roy Fisher 1930–
Toyland
Paraphrases
A Sign Illuminated

John Fuller 1930–
Daughter
Concerto for Double Bass
Valentine

Valerie Gillies 1948–
The Piano Tuner

Philip Gross 1952–
Son and Heir
From the Fast Train

Thom Gunn 1929–
Vox Humana
From the Wave
Yoko
Hide and Seek

Michael Hamburger 1924–
A Poet's Progress
Solidarity

Tony Harrison 1937–
Them & [uz]
Book Ends 1
Long Distance 2

Seamus Heaney 1939–
The Outlaw
The Skunk
Punishment
From Clearances

Geoffrey Hill 1935–
From Funeral Music 3 & 7
Merlin
Idylls of the King

Michael Hofmann 1957–
Ancient Evenings

David Holbrook 1923–
Mending the Fire
On the Brink of a Pit

Molly Holden 1927–1981
Stopping Places

Ted Hughes 1930–
Witches
Thrushes
How Water Began to Play
Roe-Deer

Elizabeth Jennings 1926–
Song at the Beginning of
Autumn
In the Night
Euthanasia

T. H. Jones 1921–1965
A Storm in Childhood

James Kirkup 1923–
No More Hiroshimas
Waiting for the Train to Start

Philip Larkin 1922–1985
Church Going
At Grass
Sad Steps
The Whitsun Weddings

James Lasdun 1958–
Bridal

Liz Lochhead 1948–
Revelation
Song of Solomon

Michael Longley 1939–
Wounds

George MacBeth 1932–
Poem for Breathing
In Love with Red
A Field of Rape

Alasdair Maclean 1936–
Rams
In Time of 'The Breaking of
Nations'
Question and Answer
Cloud shout

Derek Mahon 1944–
The Return
The Snow Party
Achill

Gerda Mayer 1927–
Sir Brooke Boothby
Lucky
Make Believe

Roger McGough 1937–
Prayer to Saint Grobianus

Medbh McGuckian 1950–
To the Nightingale

Robert Minhinnick 1952–
Short Wave
Sunday Morning

Adrian Mitchell 1932–
Fifteen Million Plastic Bags

Edwin Morgan 1920–
Strawberries
The First Men on Mercury

Blake Morrison 1956–
On Sizewell Beach

Andrew Motion 1952–
From Bloodlines: Bro
From 'This is Your Subject
Speaking'

Paul Muldoon 1951–
Cuba
Why Brownlee Left

Leslie Norris 1921–
A Glass Window
Lear at Fifty

John Ormond 1923–
My Grandfather and his
Apple Tree
The Key
Cathedral Builders

Tom Paulin 1949–
Second-Rate Republics
Pot Burial

Peter Porter 1929–
From Three Poems for Music
Mort aux Chats
An Exequy
Non Piangere, Liù

Tom Pow 1950–
Invitation

Sheenagh Pugh 1950–
'Do you think we'll ever get
to see Earth, sir?'
The Frozen Field

Craig Raine 1944–
The Behaviour of Dogs
Flying to Belfast 1977
A Martian Sends a Postcard
Home

Peter Redgrove 1932
On the Patio
Orchard with Wasps
A Scarecrow
Entry Fee

Jeremy Reed
Tulips
Buoys

Alastair Reid 1926–
The O-Filler
A Lesson in Music

Christopher Reid 1949–
Big Ideas with Loose
   Connections
A Tune

Oliver Reynolds 1957–
Thaw

Alan Ross 1922–
Stanley Matthews

Carol Rumens 1944–
Seroyeshky

Carole Satyamurti 1939–
Broken Moon
Mouthfuls

Vernon Scannell 1922–
Taken in Adultery
No Sense of Direction
I'm Covered Now
Collected Poems Recollected

Jon Silkin 1930–
Death of a Son
A Daisy

James Simmons 1933–
Claudy

C. H. Sisson 1914–
In Allusion to Propertius, I, iii
The Herb-Garden

Iain Crichton Smith 1926–
Old Woman
Two Girls Singing
By Ferry to the Island
The Chair in which you've sat

John Smith 1924–
Death at the Opera

Jon Stallworthy 1935–
A Letter from Berlin
A poem about Poems About
Vietnam

Anne Stevenson 1933–
A Daughter's Difficulties as a
Wife
Willow Song

George Szirtes 1948–
Meeting, 1944

R. S. Thomas 1913–
Welsh History
Welsh Landscape
On the Farm
Threshold

Adam Thorpe 1956–
Neighbours

Anthony Thwaite 1930–
The Bonfire
Lesson
In the Gravel Pit

Charles Tomlinson 1927–
In the Studio
Into Distance
The Journey

John Tripp 1927–1986
Connection in Bridgend
Ashes on the Cotswolds

Gael Turnbull 1928–
What Makes the Weeds Grow
Tall?

John Wain 1925–
Au Jardin des Plantes
Ode to a Nightingale

Ted Walker 1934–
New Forest Ponies

J. P. Ward 1937–
The Party
The A40 Wolvercote
Roundabout at Oxford

Andrew Waterman 1940–
In Memoriam Reggie Smith

Hugo Williams 1942–
Walking Out of the Room
Backwards

David Wright 1920–
A Funeral Oration
Monologue of a Deaf Man
By the Effigy of St Cecilia
Encounter

Kit Wright 1944–
Every Day in Every Way
Personal Advertisement
Elizabeth

INTRODUCTION

Cyril Connolly postulated that there were two kinds of literary periodicals: the dynamic and the eclectic. The dynamic, he argued, owned a strict programmatic editorial bias and so excluded the majority of talented contemporary writers, whereas the eclectic, more democratic, welcomed different stylistic modes of writing. Anthologies of contemporary poetry, it seems to me, may be classed similarly. The brief for this editor was to present the best of post-war British poetry, to include the work of those whose first books appeared between 1945 and 1988. Seemingly, then, an eclectic anthology. What is the best? Not necessarily those poets most fashionable; and since I have happily excluded some poets with considerable reputations because they fail to allow me, one fallible reader, enough enjoyment, while including others unfashionable, this eclectic anthology, I trust, is not entirely without the dynamic edge of personal bias.

To be sure, there are British poets whom I esteem whose work does not appear simply because of limited space. What is included, I believe, displays riches enough of skill and sensibility: that which arrests the reader's attention immediately and that which, amiable or harsh, needs to be pondered on.

The very word 'British' presents a problem to the anthologist. Significant contributions have been made to contemporary literature by those who have come to live and work here: Fleur Adcock was born in New Zealand, Peter Porter in Australia, James Berry in Jamaica, David Wright in South Africa and Valeries Gillies in Canada. Then there are the American-born poets, Ruth Fainlight and Anne Stevenson. Yet other poets arrived here when very young as refugees: Michael Hamburger from Germany, Gerda Mayer from Czechoslovakia and George Szirtes from Hungary.

Of late, anthologies of British poetry have emphasised the contribution made by Northern Irish poets, partly because of the undoubted talent of Seamus Heaney and others, and partly because of the tragic conflict there. Northern Irish poets have also appeared in anthologies of Irish poetry where no distinction (justly in my view) has been made between those from the South and those from the North. Indeed, if this anthology were entitled, say, 'Philip Larkin and After' rather than Post-War British Poets' then poets from the South would have found an honourable place here. As it is, there are Irish poets from the North who resent, or feel uncomfortable with, the identification-tag of 'British'. The truth is that the war in Northern Ireland belongs to the experience of both the British and the Irish and the poetry born of it may be claimed by both nations.

It may be, of course, that the very bloody circumstances in Northern Ireland have prompted critics to overstate the importance of recent poetry from that region, that the light of explosions has too sharply highlighted the silhouettes of Northern Irish makers. In any case, if I have limited the number of poems by Northern Irish poets it is in order to allow more space instead to the notable but somewhat neglected poetry emanating from Scotland and Wales.[1] Besides, urgent public engagements, other than the conflict in Ireland, have been memorably evinced and defined by post-war British poets: the menace of universal radiation, the war in Vietnam, the Falklands War, anomic anxieties engendered by recent historical catastrophes – Hiroshima and the Nazi concentration camps – as well as important, though less horrific, concerns arising from domestic political policies. Poets, though, are not journalists. They do not necessarily focus on the events of the day. They possess, or should possess, as Thomas Blackburn has suggested,[2] 'the double vision of the god, Odin'. For while one eye observes the outer scene, the other blinded eye 'beholds what is going on in the night of himself.'

---

[1]The editors of *Contemporary British Poetry* (Penguin 1982) devoted a quarter of their anthology to Northern Irish poetry. No Welsh poet was included and only one Scot.
[2]*The Price of an Eye* (Longmans Green 1961).

The poetry written in the immediate post-war years in Britain has been labelled 'Neo-romantic'. It was an hortatory poetry – wordy, ornamental, florid. The young poets of those years concentrated on being textually sensuous and gaudy and there are a few older poets to this day, Peter Redgrove among them, who continue this line. Most of those immediate post-war poets, alas, lapsed into a ludicrous grandezza, if not incoherence. Simply, they were not as gifted as their older models, Dylan Thomas and George Barker, nor as musical. By 1953, the year Dylan Thomas died, a violent reaction to Neo-romanticism was plainly evident and a new generation of young poets began to claim attention. These poets came to be known as The Movement and eventually Robert Conquest published their work in his interesting dynamic anthology *New Lines* (1956). They favoured a poetry which nurtured rationality, that was inhospitable to myth, that avoided poetic diction, that was conversationally-pitched and in opposition to Neo-romanticism. It was deliberately formal and lucid and small-gestured, regarding itself as being in the mainstream of the tactful English tradition.[3] One of their number, Kingsley Amis, wrote:

> Let us make at least visions that we need
> Let mine be pallid, so that it cannot
> Force a single glance from a single word. . .
> Let there be a path leading out of sight
> And at its other end a temperate zone:
> Woods devoid of beasts, roads that please the foot.

These poems of a temperate zone, of a slower metabolism, became popular because they reflected the atti-

[3]In *Acumen*, April 1988, Michael Hulse remarked, 'the poets we think of as having their place in a central English line – Cowper, Hardy, Edward Thomas, Sir John Betjeman, Philip Larkin'. Other critics would add other names – not least, surely, Wordsworth.

tude of a new post-war intellectual generation of writers who, sometimes nationalistically English, liked to think of themselves as tough, cynical and 'anti-wet' – a literary critical term used then and one which latterly has assumed, without difficulty, political connotations. Nationalistic or not, the Movement could count among its numbers poets genuinely talented, not least Philip Larkin. Others included in this present anthology are Elizabeth Jennings, Donald Davie, D. J. Enright, Thom Gunn and John Wain.

While the Movement poetry was ubiquitous during the 1950s other poets, less hostile to romantic modes, unashamed of rhetorical energy, were also at work, among them mavericks such as Thomas Blackburn, David Wright and Jon Silkin; and these soon after were joined by Ted Hughes, a poet also writing a differently ordered poetry from that of the Movement poets. His work, first published in 1957, received immediate acclaim. 'Ted Hughes,' wrote Edwin Muir in the *New Statesman*, 'seems to be quite outside the currents of his time.' Kingsley Amis had called for 'woods devoid of beasts'. Ted Hughes offered beasts without woods.

Nevertheless the pitch, tone, strategy, bias of the Movement poets has predominated, with modifications, to the present day. The majority of poets in this anthology whose first books were published after 1960, various as they are, would, it seems, subscribe to the main theses of the Movement aesthetic for they have appropriated the concern for propriety in the use of language. Was Samuel Johnson right when he wrote in his Preface to Shakespeare: 'If there be, what I believe there is, in every nation, a style which never becomes obsolete, a certain mode of phraseology so consonant and congenial to the analogy and principles of its respective language as to remain settled and unaltered; this style is probably to be sought in the common intercourse of life, among those who speak only to be understood.'? Be that as it may, even poets addicted to a temperate zone do, on occasions, need to speak with a greater precipitation and elegance. Few will not acknowledge, with Anacreon, that it is pleasant to be frenzied at times.

3

R. P. Blackmur, the American critic, once wrote, 'words bring meanings to birth and themselves contain the meaning as an immanent possibility before the pangs of junction.' British poets generally do not rely on a simple-minded interpretation of such a statement. It is easy to summon forth an arbitrary junction through pri-. vate association and its consequences, a meaningless or almost meaningless carnival of phrases; but this side of the Atlantic, poets prefer that junction to be strenuously worked for with a designating consciousness.[4] In the U.S.A. John Ashbery is enthroned; here Douglas Dunn can write, 'It is my contention that in contemporary writing the most ambitious goal is to be clear.'

British poetry, since the death of Dylan Thomas in 1953, has largely been ignored in the U.S.A., it being written off as too formal, over-committed to decorative rational discourse, too open to paraphrase, too suspicious of certain side-effects of Modernism (pretentiousness and empty obscurity). There are signs lately, though, of an alteration in American critical bias. It seems many younger American poets are themselves in revolt and their work has become not only more lucid but more aurally alert.[5] A New American Formalism has been signalled and discussed in several critical articles, most notably by Dana Gioia in *The Hudson Review* and by Alan Shapiro in *Critical Inquiry*.

Even an anthology of so-called rhymed and metred verse, *The Direction of Poetry*, has been published, edited

[4]British exceptions include the Northern Irish poet, Medbh McGuckian.
[5]Gjertrud Schnackenberg and Michael Donaghy are two formal younger American poets who have recently been published in Britain. Both, deservedly, have received acclaim.

by Robert Richman. Thus in some influential quarters the sterility of American hermetic formless verse is under attack as is 'a joylessly intellectual approach'. What is offered instead are smaller-gestured but delight-giving aural modes. Dana Gioia could be a post-war British poet when he advocates:

> The music that of common speech
> but slanted so that each detail
> sounds unexpected as a sharp
> inserted in a simple scale.
>
> No jumble box of imagery
> dumped glumly in the reader's lap
> or elegantly packaged junk
> the unsuspecting must unwrap,
>
> But words that could direct a friend
> precisely to an unknown place . . .

Accompanying these uncorybantic and more formal strategies is a greater curiosity about the paradigm of Post-War British Poetry which this present anthology, I trust, will help to serve and satisfy.

Not that we should be too self-congratulatory about the poetry that has been published during the post-war years this side of the Atlantic. Alan Shapiro, referring to the New American Formalism, states an obvious truth when he judges that formal verse can be as dull as experimental verse when both own 'a complacency of language and detail' and when metrical technique is mechanically related to the theme. There is no shortage of dull work being produced both sides of the Atlantic, even though we, more than the Americans, have paid attention in latter years to traditional metrical devices. It cannot be denied that we are particularly skilful at writing verse – comic (John Fuller's 'Valentine' or poems by Kit Wright and Wendy Cope), poignant (Tony Harrison), politically passionate (James Fenton, Adrian Mitchell) and even that which aspires to poetry rather than verse frequently dispenses also with the pomp of artificial diction and, verbally, can be misleadingly low-keyed as in the work of Patricia Beer or Andrew Motion. Perhaps the clarities and occasional class preoccupations of poets such as Douglas Dunn and Tony Harrison are what Americans expect from typical British poetry. Certainly poetry in Britain, more than in the U.S.A., has a constituency outside the Universities and this may be one reason why British poets are audacious enough to pitch their voices in a more frontal manner. Some have gone too far in this direction, their verse becoming over-explicit and, for the most part, fit merely for oral performance. Others, though, have remained deliberately suggestive, like Geoffrey Hill, or attempted to see the minutiae of the world as if they were without prior knowledge, like Craig Raine.[6] Despite this variety, most poets in this anthology could be defined, more or less, as the modern heirs to Wordsworth or rather to the theoretical author of the second edition of the Lyrical Ballads where he remarked, 'The principal object, then, proposed in these poems was to choose incidents and situations from common life, and to relate or describe them throughout, as far as was possible, in a selection of language really used by men and, at the same time, to throw over them a certain colouring of the imagination, whereby ordinary things should be presented to the mind in an unusual aspect; and further, and above all, to make these incidents and situations interesting by tracing in them, truly though not ostentatiously, the primary laws of our nature . . .'

What Wordsworth demanded first from poetry was pleasure, the poem's 'necessity of producing immediate pleasure'; and what has guided me in my choice of poetry for this anthology has been the capacity of poems to propagate pleasure in all its subtle combinations of intellect and feeling, poems that can be read – to paraphrase Wordsworth – repeatedly where prose may be read but

[6]The so-called 'Martian poetry' is exemplified in this anthology not only by Craig Raine but by John Fuller ('Concerto for Double Bass'), Jeremy Reed ('Buoys' and 'Tulips'), and by Christopher Reid ('Big Ideas with Loose Connections').

once. Among the poems published here some will be known to inveterate poetry readers, others probably quite unfamiliar; and I have on occasions deliberately chosen poems by different poets which, because of similar themes and scenes, invite comparison with each other. I believe the pleasure from reading them in tandem can be synergistically enhanced. Thus James Kirkup's 'No More Hiroshimas' and Adrian Mitchell's 'Fifteen Million Bags' can be bracketed together, as can Ted Hughes's 'Roe Deer' and Ted Walker's 'New Forest Ponies'; Ursula Fanthorpe's 'Soothing and Awful' and Philip Larkin's 'Church Going'; John Cassidy's 'Attitude of Mind' and Anthony Thwaite's 'In the Gravel Pit'; D. J. Enright's 'Abbey Going' and the extract from Andrew Motion's 'This is Your Subject Speaking' – as well as many others.

I hope this anthology will outlast the transient authority of fashion and temporary critical opinion so that, in a later edition, I shall be able to amend it and add to its contents poems from the youngest poets who have only recently made, or are about to make, their publishing debuts. Meanwhile, this editor will be disappointed if the reader – British, American or whoever, expert or neophyte – does not discover here many poems that will repose in his or her mind for years to come and that, lastly, he or she will be attracted to books by individual poets as a result. For in such an eclectic anthology as this, poets can only be teasingly sampled and enjoyed.

For a Five-year-old

A snail is climbing up the window-sill
Into your room, after a night of rain.
You call me in to see, and I explain
That it would be unkind to leave it there:
It might crawl to the floor; we must take care
That no one squashes it. You understand,
And carry it outside, with careful hand,
To eat a daffodil.

I see, then, that a kind of faith prevails:
Your gentleness is moulded still by words
From me, who have trapped mice and shot wild birds,
From me, who drowned your kittens, who betrayed
Your closest relatives, and who purveyed
The harshest kind of truth to many another.
But that is how things are: I am your mother,
And we are kind to snails.

Leaving the Tate

Coming out with your clutch of postcards
in a Tate Gallery bag and another clutch
of images packed into your head you pause
on the steps to look across the river

and there's a new one: light bright buildings,
a streak of brown water, and such a sky
you wonder who painted it – Constable? No:
too brilliant. Crome? No: too ecstatic –

a madly pure Pre-Raphaelite sky,
perhaps, sheer blue apart from the white plumes
rushing up it (today, that is,
April. Another day would be different

1

but it wouldn't matter. All skies work.)
Cut to the lower right for a detail:
seagulls pecking on mud, below
two office blocks and a Georgian terrace.

Now swing to the left, and take in plane-trees
bobbled with seeds, and that brick building,
and a red bus . . . Cut it off just there,
by the lamp-post. Leave the scaffolding in.

That's your next one. Curious how
these outdoor pictures didn't exist
before you'd looked at the indoor pictures,
the ones on the walls. But here they are now,

marching out of their panorama
and queuing up for the viewfinder
your eye's become. You can isolate them
by holding your optic muscles still.

You can zoom in on figure studies
(that boy with the rucksack), or still lives,
abstracts, townscapes. No one made them.
The light painted them. You're in charge

of the hanging committee. Put what space
you like around the ones you fix on,
and gloat. Art multiplies itself.
Art's whatever you choose to frame.

Future Work

'Please send future work'
                    —Editor's note on a rejection slip.

It is going to be a splendid summer.
The apple tree will be thick with golden russets
expanding weightily in the soft air.

2

I shall finish the brick wall beside the terrace
and plant out all the geranium cuttings.
Pinks and carnations will be everywhere.

She will come out to me in the garden,
her bare feet pale on the cut grass,
bringing jasmine tea and strawberries on a tray.
I shall be correcting the proofs of my novel
(third in a trilogy – simultaneous publication
in four continents); and my latest play

will be in production at the Aldwych
starring Glenda Jackson and Paul Scofield
with Olivier brilliant in a minor part.
I shall probably have finished my translations
of Persian creation myths and the Pre-Socratics
(drawing new parallels) and be ready to start

on Lucretius. But first I'll take a break
at the chess championships in Manila –
on present form, I'm fairly likely to win.
And poems? Yes, there will certainly be poems:
they sing in my head, they tingle along my nerves.
It is all magnificently about to begin.

The Bullaun

'Drink water from the hollow in the stone . . .'
This was it, then – the cure for madness:
A rock with two round cavities, filled with rain;
A thing I'd read about once, and needed, then,
But since forgotten. I didn't expect it here –
Not having read the guidebook;
Not having planned, even, to be in Antrim.
'There's a round tower, isn't there?' I'd asked.
The friendly woman in the post office
Gave me directions: 'Up there past the station,
Keep left, on a way further – it's a fair bit –

And have you been to Lough Neagh yet?' I walked –
It wasn't more than a mile – to the stone phallus
Rising above its fuzz of beech-trees
In the municipal gardens. And beside it,
This. I circled around them,
Backing away over wet grass and beechmast,
Aiming the camera (since I had it with me,
Since I was playing tourist this afternoon)
And saw two little boys pelting across.
'Take our photo! Take our photo! Please!'
We talked it over for a bit –
How I couldn't produce one then and there;
But could I send it to them with the postman?
Well, could they give me their addresses?
Kevin Tierney and Declan McCallion,
Tobergill Gardens. I wrote, they stood and smiled,
I clicked, and waved goodbye, and went.
Two miles away, an hour later,
Heading dutifully through the damp golf-course
To Lough Neagh, I thought about the rock,
Wanting it. Not for my own salvation;
Hardly at all for me: for sick Belfast,
For the gunmen and the slogan-writers,
For the poor crazy girl I met in the station,
For Kevin and Declan, who would soon mistrust
All camera-carrying strangers. But of course
The thing's already theirs: a monument,
A functionless, archaic, pitted stone
And a few mouthfuls of black rainwater.

The Faithful Wife

I am away from home
A hundred miles from the blue curtains
I made at Christmas and the table
My grandfather brought back from Sorrento.
I am a career woman at a conference.
I love my husband. I value
Both what I own and what I do.

I left the forsythias half yellow,
The bluebells – lifted from a wood in Suffolk
Last year – still tight, the mint surfacing.
I must sweep the paths when I get back.

And here for the past week you and I
Have been conducting a non-affair
That could not even be called flirtation
That could not be called anything
Except unusually straightforward desire,
Adultery in the heart.
Life is so short.

The programme is ending.
11.30 – Conference disperses.
I watch everybody leaving.
It feels like grief, like the guillotine.

Your turn now; go home
With the 'Good-bye, love'
You use to every personable woman.
Get in your large car which ten years ago
Was full of sand and children's things
On summer evenings.
You are middle-aged now, as I am.
Write your notes up,

Fix the rattling window,
Keep your marriage vows. As I shall.

The Letter

I have not seen your writing
For ages, nor have been fretting
To see it. As once, darling.

This letter will certainly be
About some book, written by you or by me.
You turned to other ghosts. So did I.

It stopped raining long ago
But drops caught up in the bough
Fall murderously on me now.

JAMES BERRY

Lucy's Letter

Things harness me here. I long
for we labrish* bad. Doors
not fixed open here.
No Leela either. No Cousin
Lil, Miss Lottie or Bro'-Uncle.
Dayclean doesn' have cockcrowin'.
Midmornin' doesn' bring
Cousin-Maa with her naseberry tray.
Afternoon doesn' give a ragged
Manwell, strung with fish
like bright leaves. Seven days
play same note in London, chile.
But Leela, money-rustle regular.

Me dear, I don' laugh now,
not'n' like we thunder claps
in darkness on verandah.
I turned a battery hen
in 'lectric light, day an' night.
No mood can touch one
mango season back at Yard.
At least though I did start
evening school once.
An' doctors free, chile.

London isn' like we
village dirt road, you know
Leela: it a parish
of pasture-lan' what
grown crisscross streets,
an' they lie down to my door.
But I lock myself in.
I carry keys everywhere.
Life here's no open summer,

girl. But Sat'day mornin' don'
find me hand' dry, don' find me face
a heavy cloud over the man.

An' though he still have
a weekend mind for bat'n'ball
he wash a dirty dish now, me dear.
It sweet him I on the Pill.
We get money for holidays
but there's no sun-hot
to enjoy cool breeze.

Leela, I really a sponge
you know, for traffic noise,
for work noise, for halfway
intentions, for halfway smiles,
for clockwatchin' an' col' weather.
I hope you don' think I gone
too fat when we meet.
I booked up to come an' soak
the children in daylight.

*(Labrish: to gossip without restraint.)

THOMAS BLACKBURN

Teaching Wordsworth

I'm paid to speak, and money glosses
Irrelevance; to keep their places
Students are paid, and so the burden
Is lightened of our mutual boredom,
And if the gain's not much the damage
Is also slight within this college.

Since for the most part it's subjective,
Verse is not anything you might have
In hand or a bank, although it is
Important to some (it is on our syllabus)
Concerned with life's outgoing towards death.
Our theme today is the poet, Wordsworth.

Who, since not alive still, I disinter
For the sake of a question you will answer,
For the sake also of the vagrant lives
He was involved with, and the wind when it raves
Round such unmarketable places as Scafell.
An unsociable man and often dull,

He lived for a long time posthumous
To the 'flashing shield', to the poet he was,
Busy for the most part with pedestrian exercise;
However you will not be questioned on those days,
Only the time when with stone footfall
Crags followed him, winds blew through his long skull.

That, of course, is known as 'the Great Period'.
Though one hesitates to apply the word 'God'
To a poet's theme – it is so manhandled –
Gentlemen, I can offer you nothing instead;
If he himself never applied it to what occurred
When 'the light of sense went out' this useful word

Though inaccurate will cut my lecture short
Being the full-stop which ends thought

And consequently for our purpose useful;
For its brevity you should be grateful.
Anyway for those who 'know' what the man meant,
My words are – thanks to God – irrelevant.
Take notes is the advice I bequeath the rest;
It is a question of self-interest,

Of being, as Shakespeare says, 'to oneself true',
Since the right marks will certainly benefit you.
After all, in the teaching world, exam and thesis
For the better posts provide a sound basis,
And in this sense poems are as good as money.
This man's life was a strange journey.

Early deprived of both father and mother,
To the rocks he turned, to lapping water,
With a sense by deprivation made so acute
That he heard grass speak and the word in a stone's
                                                    throat;
Many, of course, to silence address their prayer,
But in his case when he spoke it chose to answer,

And he wrote down, after a certain time-lag,
Their conversation. It is a dialogue
Almost unique in any literature
And a positive gold-mine to the commentator,
For although his words mention what silence said
It can almost any way be interpreted,

Since to find a yardstick by which the occult
Language of stones can be measured is difficult,
Also that 'something far more deeply interfused'
Must be belittled by critiques, if not abused,
There being no instrument with which to measure
This origin of terms and formula

10

Which, together with the birth and deathward aim
Of the life in us and things, was this man's theme,
As he grew and dwindled into a worse
End of life (as regards verse).
My conclusion is: most words do violence
To what he said, Listen to silence.

Francis Bacon

The crumpled sheets of the bed of murder
You showed me how the creases, stains and folds
Make the crime perpetually occur,
The resonance and the mystery of details.

I remember the chaos of cuttings and paint,
The colours on the plate in your studio,
How you called Jesus a queen but very quaint.
I disagreed but agreed with your cult of horror.

And collected pictures in an old scrap book,
A dying drunk, boxers, an addict of heroin,
Many variants on the theme of pain and shock;
I shudder at them now, they were pleasant then.

Degradation, not degraded yourself, your fascination
All the varieties of misery and mania;
You called it closing in to the nerve; I leant upon
The enormity of the creature that you are

And made poems underneath your cast shadow,
Exploring the terror of bearing humanity
And relishing – what it was I still don't know,
Something about breaking out of contour into mystery.

Now at sixty-one and having learnt compassion,
Some insight from confusion and despair
I seek the pities, how to make confusion
Both in myself and others breathe fresher air

11

And marvel at you very rich and famous,
Still crucified by what takes place in a bed,
And uttering, with superb technique, pretentious
Platitudes of rut, that you have said and said.

Laudanum

For a raging tooth, a bad cold or neuralgia
It was prescribed constantly and thought benevolent
By many eminent professors of Medicare;
Mind you, as regards children, to sleep full
Of Mother Bailey's Spirit or McMums Elixir –
Though good for dinner parties, could be lethal –
And often was. For the poor, cheaper than gin,
It relieved the pain of being human
Under inhuman conditions. Wealthier, poetic men,
Whether the stimulus was cholera or insomnia
Celebrated their first rapport like a honeymoon.
Ecstatic visions rewarded the enquirer
In a passive sense, for the most part, beautiful
Enough in itself. The mooned and poppied water
The basin of the mind itself could fill
And dispense with the ardour of the creator;
Only from far off, the dumb blind waiter
Groped from eternity to present the bill.

ALISON BRACKENBURY

Gallop

An unholy conspiracy
of girls and horses, I admit,
as never being part in it
but riding late and anxiously.
On Sunday when the horses climb the hill
scrambling the dired watercourse to reach
the open field to gallop: all my breath
swells hot inside me as the horses bunch
and pull for mad speed, even my old horse –

'gently!' the leader calls – but they are gone,
hunters, young horses, surging hard ahead,
I rocked across the saddle, the wet soil
flung shining past me, and the raking feet
shaking me from stirrups as I speak
breathless, kind names to the tossing neck
haul back the reins, watching the widening gap
between my foundered horse and the fast pack,

wondering if I can keep on, why I do this;
and as he falters, my legs tired as his,
I faintly understand the rage for speed:
careless and hard, what do they see ahead,
galloping down spring's white light, but a gate
a neat house, a small lawn, a cage of sunlight?

And pounding, slow, behind, I wish that I
rode surely as they do but wish I could
tell them what I see in sudden space –
Two flashing magpies rising from the trees
two birds: good omen; how the massive cloud
gleams and shadows over as they wait,
the horses blown and steaming at shut gates:
disclosing, past their bright heads, my dark wood.

EDWIN BROCK

Song of the Battery Hen

We can't grumble about accommodation:
we have a new concrete floor that's
always dry, four walls that are
painted white, and a sheet-iron roof
the rain drums on. A fan blows warm air
beneath our feet to disperse the smell
of chicken-shit and, on dull days,
fluorescent lighting sees us.

You can tell me: if you come by
the North door, I am in the twelfth pen
on the left-hand side of the third row
from the floor; and in that pen
I am usually the middle one of three.
But, even without directions, you'd
discover me. I have the same orange-
red comb, yellow beak and auburn
feathers, but as the door opens and you
hear above the electric fan a kind of
one-word wail, I am the one
who sounds loudest in my head.

Listen. Outside this house there's an
orchard with small moss-green apple
trees; beyond that, two fields of
cabbages; then, on the far side of
the road, a broiler house. Listen:
one cockerel grows out of there, as
tall and proud as the first hour of sun.
Sometimes I stop calling with the others
to listen, and wonder if he hears me.

The next time you come here, look for me.
Notice the way I sound inside my head.
God made us all quite differently,
and blessed us with this expensive home.

GEORGE MACKAY BROWN

Ikey on the People of Hellya

Rognvald who stalks round Corse with his stick
I do not love.
His dog has a loud sharp mouth.
The wood of his door is very hard.
Once, tangled in his barbed wire
(I was paying respects to his hens, stroking a wing)
He laid his stick on me.
That was out of a hard forest also.

Mansie at Quoy is a biddable man.
Ask for water, he gives you rum.
I strip his scarecrow April by April.
Ask for a scattering of straw in his byre
He lays you down
Under a quilt as long and light as heaven.
Then only his raging woman spoils our peace.

Gray the fisherman is no trouble now
Who quoted me the vagrancy laws
In a voice slippery as seaweed under the kirkyard.
I rigged his boat with the seven curses.
Occasionally still, for encouragement,
I put the knife in his net.

Though she has black peats and a yellow hill
And fifty silken cattle
I do not go near Merran and her cats.
Rather break a crust on a tombstone.
Her great-great-grandmother
Wore the red coat at Gallowsha.

The thousand rabbits of Hollandsay
Keep Simpson's corn short,
Whereby comes much cruelty, gas and gunshot.

Tonight I have lit a small fire.
I have stained my knife red.
I had peeled a round turnip.
And I pray the Lord
To preserve those nine hundred and ninety-nine
                                        innocent.

Finally in Folscroft lives Jeems,
Tailor and undertaker, a crosser of limbs,
One tape for the living and the dead.
He brings a needle to my rags in winter,
And he guards, against my stillness
The seven white boards
I got from the Danish wreck one winter.

Love Letter

To Mistress Madeline Richan, widow
At Quoy, parish of Voes, in the time of hay:

   The old woman sat in her chair, mouth
                                agape
   At the end of April.
   There were buttercups in a jar in
                        the window.

   The floor is not a blue mirror now
   And the table has flies and bits of
                                crust on it.
   Also the lamp glass is broken.

   I have the shop at the end of the
                        house
   With sugar, tea, tobacco, paraffin
   And, for whisperers, a cup of whisky.

   There is a cow, a lady of butter, in
                        the long silk grass
   And seven sheep on Moorfea.

17

The croft girls are too young.
Nothing but giggles, lipstick, and
                              gramophone records.

Walk over the hill Friday evening.
Enter without knocking
If you see one red rose in the window.

ALAN BROWNJOHN

Office Party

We were throwing out small-talk
On the smoke-weary air,
When the girl with the squeaker
Came passing each chair.

She was wearing a white dress,
Her paper-hat was a blue
Crown with a red tassel,
And to every man who

Glanced up at her, she leant over
And blew down the hole,
So the squeaker inflated
And began to unroll.

She stopped them all talking
With this trickery,
And she didn't leave out anyone
Until she came to me.

I looked up and she met me
With a half-teasing eye
And she took a mild breath and
Went carefully by,

And with cold concentration
To the next man she went,
And squawked out the instrument
To its fullest extent.

And whether she passed me
Thinking that it would show
Too much favour to mock me
I never did know –

Or whether her withholding
Was her cruelty,
And it was that she despised me,
I couldn't quite see –

So it could have been discretion,
And it could have been disgust,
But it was quite unequivocal,
And suffer it I must:

All I know was: she passed me,
Which I did not expect
– And I'd never so craved for
Some crude disrespect.

Formosavej

The tramway ran out along into the night,
Its rails were wet from the rain and the tramway
                                  continued.
It met houses, it met shops, it met parks, it met cafés,
It met dogs.

              And in the shining of
The light of the lamps in the rain on its tracks
It went steadily on with its own quiet, metal
Wilfulness all the time.

              On it, the brittle
Narrow, bright, single-decker trams rang and
Rattled: busy and green-grey frameworks
Of glitter and rightness.

              At the many turns
In the wide streets and the by-streets their
Brakes drew in breath and groaned, at
Jolts and bumps on the track all the dainty
Lights went off and came on again.

Overhead, through all this,
The wires droned and thudded and crackled
And at sudden halts all the empty red-leather
Seats reversed themselves.

When the terminus came,
It was a splendid aggregation of trams on
The circle of tracks at the end of the route,
A stupefying, fascinating, memorable
                Clatter of numbers

And lights and signs and conductors and drivers
And cheerful spitting sparks at the knots
In the overhead wires. Readers, you would have
                Enjoyed this as much as I did.

In a Restaurant

The facing mirrors showed two rooms
Which rhymed and balanced beautifully,
So everything we wore and ate
Shone doubly clear for you and me.

In the next image after that
Life seemed the same in every way:
Green bottles and white tablecloths
And cutlery as clean as day;

But in the third, things looked a mite
Less brilliant than in the first two . . .
A sort of mist was falling on
The features of a dwindling view,

And by the time our gaze had gone
Searching down to rooms eight and nine,
The world seemed darker, and confused,
Its outlines harder to define,

Its faces tinier. There, instead
Of warmth and clarity and bright
Colours for everything, we saw
A shadow land, a listless light

Which neither of us understood:
A place so closed and small and black
It nearly hurt, smiling, gripping
Our glasses harder, coming back.

MICHAEL BURN

In Japan

In Japan the poets write to each other:
'I wish I could write like you.
I go on dabbing at screens with my tired brushwork.
Yours is so brave and new.'

In Japan the poets reply to each other:
    'The first polish of words is mine,
Which produces a mist. The second (Esteemed Sir)
Is yours, which makes them shine.'

In Japan the poets cable the critics:
'Disgusted at line you took
About my latest stop how dare honoured sir
Recommend so worthless book.'

In Japan the poets wrote to the editors:
'Thanks for returning enclosure
To this insignificant person, thereby
Saving him public exposure.'

In Japan the poets say to the public:
    'Thank you for being immense.
I refund in part for poems that have no rhythm.
In full if they have no sense.'

And publishers receive verses
In paint on a feathered fan:
'This humble singer rejoices in those you left out.'
That's how it is in Japan.

An Attitude of Mind

Heat bounced off the cobbled yard
And hit us in the eyes, already bleared
By the sun to a constant blink.
Starlings showered down onto the barn,
Dipped through the door, paused, and sprayed up
    again,
Ceaselessly. Dust twirled slowly; a tractor stank.

Tod took a tennis racket, and flicked
It from hand to hand. You've picked
A good time, he said. I'll demonstrate.
The barn was heavy with hay smell
And all in it invisible
When Tod swung the doors together, tight.

In the dimness hovered small echoings,
The whirring motors of starlings' wings,
Soft and confusing, and right up,
Where the nests were, raucous twitters.
We stood till things assembled round us,
Colouring themselves and taking shape:

A spiked machine, blue plastic sacks
Of nitro-chalk, a couple of hayforks,
A three-wheeled pram. Heavy beams
Hung over us, streaked white like the walls
Up at the top amid squalls
Of bird noise. Tod flung wide his arms

And shook his muscles loose, and took
A good grip on his racket. With a kick
He broke some pebbles free, and flung one
Up at the roof, then another, then more,

And they clunked about on the wood up there
Before the sharp drop back onto stone.

And down came the starlings, beating about
In a bewildered way, at head height and waist height,
Dozens of them, whizzing so close they missed
Us by the width of their wind. Tod was using
The racket, swinging from the shoulder, not pausing
At all, grunting and moving very fast.

Blow after blow vibrated those strings.
Bodies rocketed to stillness, and there were shufflings
And dragging movements everywhere,
As birds, beaks broken, necks half-unscrewed,
Flapped untidily and slowly clawed
A small circular progress on the floor.

Tod stamped on these but others escaped to the roof
In the end and sat safe. Tod gave a laugh
At his last few futile swipes and looked
Round at the litter of feathers, at the wrecks
Of birds and bits of birds, at the marks
On the walls where birds had split and cracked.

The nearest bodies he nudged with the toe of his boot
To a neat heap, and he scooped with his racket
Several more to throw in; he was deft, accurate.
Hungry nests wheezed still. They'll soon starve,
That lot, Tod said, stroking his car with the curve
Of his racket. Tomorrow in here will be dead quiet.

He opened the doors and the daylight fell
In, hot and dazzling. A good haul,
He said, licking sweat, wiping an eye, puzzled
At my silence. Pests they are from the minute they
                                        hatch.
It's all an attitude of mind. He raised an arm to scratch.
Down the words Dunlop Junior dark blood drizzled.

Frozen Canal

After three days of frost a boy on a bike
Is daringly first to prove the black

Top of the iced canal a highway now,
Slick between banks off-white with old snow.

Dodging a bottle buried to its snout
And an iceberg tyre one-ninth out

He spins with an Indian whoop under a bridge
Past his companions fringing the timid edge,

And they follow, all of them, to ride and skitter and
    glide
Along the hissing crown of this new road.

Then a heavy drumming in the frosted air
Brings the butting shoulders of the ice-breaker,

The spoil-sport barge labouring to thump and crack
Leaving brick-sized ice-blocks jumbled in its wake.

Deliberate this. Under unreflecting ice
The sepia water waits for a shocked face

To splinter and blunder in, waits for a mouth
It can fill with sludge to silence, throttling the breath.

It happens – often enough for a barge to be sent
Whenever the ice will hold a footstep, blunt

Prow pushing the games away to the thrum
Of diesels. The boys stand with their beached bike,
    dumb

Till the devastating passage has rumbled through,
Then shrilling at the helmsman, hurling futile snow.

But he, indifferent, steers on his ordered track,
While they, saved, desolated, swear at his crouched
    back.

Disturbance

I woke when a magpie hammered
Its machine-gun voice from close range
Into my ear as if in the same room.
A sharp light marked the first break
Of the first morning in June, the sky
A whole smooth eggshell.

The magpie was smashing a sparrow's nest
Above the window, pick-axing through
To the bald, reptilian young.
Three days hatched, they were spiked
Out of that lined, close world by a black
Bill and an implacable eye.

All their last energy went in a frenzy
Of wheezing. One was lifted fifty yards
Away to a bough and banged and broken
And gulped. It was there to be seen but I saw
In my mind and lay close under blankets
Unmoving, thinking of instability

And how it seems to live in another
Medium, unseen, unknown, outside,
Till the great beak crashes in.
Knowing it is no benefit, I hear
The black-white-black flap of that magpie
Come chattering back for the next grab.

CHARLES CAUSLEY

Ou Phrontis
(*to E. M. Forster*)

The bells assault the maiden air,
The coachman waits with a carriage and pair,
But the bridegroom says *I won't be there,*
    I don't care!

Three times three times the banns declare
That the boys may blush and the girls may glare,
But the bridegroom is occupied elsewhere,
    I don't care!

Lord, but the neighbours all will stare,
Their temperatures jump as high as a hare,
But the bridegroom says *I've paid my fare,*
    I don't care!

The bride she waits by the bed so bare,
Soft as a pillow is her hair,
But the bridegroom jigs with the leg of a chair,
    I don't care!

Say, but her father's a millionaire,
A girdle of gold all night will she wear,
You must your foolish ways forswear.
    I don't care!

Her mother will offer, if she dare,
A ring that is rich but not so rare
If you'll keep your friendship in repair.
    I don't care!

Her sisters will give you a plum and a pear
And a diamond saddle for your mare.
O bridegroom! For the night prepare!
    I don't care!

Her seven brothers all debonair
Will do your wishes and some to spare
If from your fancy you'll forbear.
    I don't care!

Say, but a maid you wouldn't scare
Now that you've got her in your snare?
And what about your son and heir?
    I don't care!

She'll leap, she'll leap from the highest stair,
She'll drown herself in the river there.
With the silver knife her flesh she'll tear.
    I don't care!

Then another will lie in the silken lair
And cover with kisses her springing hair.
Another the bridal bed will share.
    I don't care!

I shall stand on my head on the table bare,
I shall kick my lily-white legs in the air,
I shall wash my hands of the whole affair,
    I don't care!

Family Feeling

My Uncle Alfred had the terrible temper.
Wrapped himself up in its invisible cloak.
When the mood was on, his children crept from the
                                            kitchen.
It might have been mined. Not even the budgie spoke.

He was killed in the First World War in Mesopotamia.
His widow rejoiced, though she never wished him
                                            dead.
After three years a postcard arrived from Southampton.
'Coming home Tuesday. Alf,' was what it said.

His favourite flower he called the antimirrhinum.
Grew it instead of greens on the garden plot.
Didn't care much for children, though father of seven.
Owned in his lifetime nine dogs all called Spot.

At Carnival time he rode the milkman's pony.
Son of the Sheikh, a rifle across his knee.
Alf the joiner as Peary in cotton-wool snowstorms.
Secret in cocoa and feathers, an Indian Cree.

I recognized him once as the Shah of Persia.
My Auntie's front-room curtains gave him away.
'It's Uncle Alf!' I said, but his glance was granite.
'Mind your own business, nosey,' I heard him say.

I never knew just what it was that bugged him,
Or what kind of love a father's love could be.
One by one his children bailed out of the homestead.
'You were too young when yours died,' they explained
                                                    to me.

Today, walking through St Cyprian's Church-yard
I saw where he lay in a box the dry colour of bone.
The grass was tamed and trimmed as if for a Sunday.
Seven antimirrhinums in a jar of stone.

Timothy Winters

Timothy Winters comes to school
With eyes as wide as a football-pool,
Ears like bombs and teeth like splinters:
A blitz of a boy is Timothy Winters.

His belly is white, his neck is dark,
And his hair is an exclamation-mark.
His clothes are enough to scare a crow
And through his britches the blue winds blow.

30

When teacher talks he won't hear a word
And he shoots down dead the arithmetic-bird,
He licks the patterns off his plate
And he's not even heard of the Welfare State.

Timothy Winters has bloody feet
And he lives in a house on Suez Street,
He sleeps in a sack on the kitchen floor
And they say there aren't boys like him any more.

Old Man Winters likes his beer
And his missus ran off with a bombardier,
Grandma sits in the grate with a gin
And Timothy's dosed with an aspirin.

The Welfare Worker lies awake
But the law's as tricky as a ten-foot snake,
So Timothy Winters drinks his cup
And slowly goes on growing up.

At Morning Prayers the Master helves
For children less fortunate than ourselves,
And the loudest response in the room is when
Timothy Winters roars 'Amen!'

So come one angel, come on ten:
Timothy Winters says 'Amen
Amen amen amen amen.'
Timothy Winters, Lord.

                              Amen.

GILLIAN CLARKE

The Hare
(*for Frances Horovitz*)

That March night I remember how we heard
a baby crying in a neighbouring room
but found him sleeping quietly in his cot.

The others went to bed and we sat late
talking of children and the men we loved.
You thought you'd like another child. 'Too late'

you said. And we fell silent, thought a while
of yours with his copper hair and mine,
a grown daughter and sons.

Then, that joke we shared, our phases of the moon.
'Sisterly lunacy' I said. You liked
the phrase. It became ours. Different

as earth and air, yet in one trace that week
we towed the calends like boats reining
the oceans of the world at the full moon.

Suddenly from the fields we heard again
a baby cry, and standing at the door
listened for minutes, ears and eyes soon used

to the night. It was cold. In the east
the river made a breath of shining sound.
The cattle in the field were shadow black.

A cow coughed. Some slept and some pulled grass.
I could smell blossom from the blackthorn
and see their thorny crowns against the sky.

And then again, a sharp cry from the hill.
'A hare', we said together, not speaking
of fox or trap that held it in a lock

of terrible darkness. Both admitted,
next day, to lying guilty hours awake
at the crying of the hare. You told me

of sleeping at last in the jaws of a bad dream.
'I saw all the suffering of the world
in a single moment. Then I heard

a voice say "But this is nothing, nothing
to the mental pain".' I couldn't speak of it.
I thought about your dream when you lay ill.

In the last heavy nights before full moon,
when its face seems sorrowful and broken,
I look through binoculars. Its seas flower

like clouds over water, it wears its craters
like silver rings. Even in dying you
menstruated as a woman in health

considering to have a child or no.
When they hand me insults or little hurts
and I'm on fire with my arguments

at your great distance you can calm me still.
Your dream, my sleeplessness, the cattle
asleep under a full moon,

and out there
the dumb and stiffening body of the hare.

Overheard in County Sligo

I married a man from County Roscommon
and I live at the back of beyond
with a field of cows and a yard of hens
and six white geese on the pond.

At my door's a square of yellow corn
caught up by its corners and shaken,
and the road runs down through the open gate
and freedom's there for the taking.

I had thought to work on the Abbey stage
or have my name in a book,
to see my thought on the printed page,
or still the crowd with a look.

But I turn to fold the breakfast cloth
and to polish the lustre and brass,
to order and dust the tumbled rooms
and find my face in the glass.

I ought to feel I'm a happy woman
for I lie in the lap of the land,
and I married a man from County Roscommon
and I live in the back of beyond.

STEWART CONN

Farm Funeral

His hearse should have been drawn by horses.
That's what he envisaged: the strain
And clop of crupper and chain, flashing
Brass, fetlocks forcing high. With below
Him, the frayed sheets turning slowly yellow.

On the sideboard a silver cup he had won,
Inscribed 'to Todd Cochrane', now a lamp;
And tinted prints of his trotting days:
Switch in hand, jockey-capped, the gig silky
With light, wheels exquisitely spinning.

For fifty years he was a breeder of horses;
Nursing them nightly, mulling soft praise
Long after the vet would have driven his plunger in.
Yet through them was his hip split. Twice
He was crushed by a stallion rearing.

Himself to the end unbroken. God's tool, yes,
That to earth will return. But not before time . . .
He ought to have been conveyed to the grave
By clattering Clydesdales – not cut off
From lark and sorrel by unseemly glass.

The shire is sprinkled with his ashes.
The fields are green through his kind. Their clay,
His marrow. As much as the roisterer, he: even
That last ride to Craigie, boots tightly laced,
His tie held in place by a diamond pin.

Visiting Hour

In the pond of our new garden
were five orange stains, under
inches of ice. Weeks since anyone
had been there. Already by far
the most severe winter for years.
You broke the ice with a hammer.
I watched the goldfish appear,
blunt-nosed and delicately clear.

Since then so much has taken place
to distance us from what we were.
That it should come to this.
Unable to hide the horror
in my eyes, I stand helpless
by your bedside and can do no more
than wish it were simply a matter
of smashing the ice and giving you air.

TONY CONRAN

Elegy for the Welsh Dead, in the Falkland Islands, 1982

Gŵyr a aeth Gatraeth oedd ffraeth eu llu.
Glasfedd eu hancwyn, a gwenwyn fu.
                    – *Y Gododdin* (6th century)
(Men went to Catraeth, keen was their company.
They were fed on fresh mead, and it proved poison.)

Men went to Catraeth. The luxury liner
For three weeks feasted them.
They remembered easy ovations,
Our boys, splendid in courage.
For three weeks the albatross roads,
Passwords of dolphin and petrel,
Practised their obedience
Where the killer whales gathered,
Where the monotonous seas yelped.
Though they went to church with their standards
Raw death has them garnished.

Men went to Catraeth. The Malvinas
Of their destiny greeted them strangely.
Instead of affection there was coldness,
Splintering iron and the icy sea,
Mud and the wind's malevolent satire.
They stood nonplussed in the bomb's indictment.

Malcolm Wigley of Connah's Quay. Did his helm
Ride high in the war-line?
Did he drink enough mead for that journey?
The desolated shores of Tegeingl,
Did they pig this steel that destroyed him?
The Dee runs silent beside empty foundries.
The way of the wind and the rain is adamant.

Clifford Elley of Pontypridd. Doubtless he feasted.
He went to Catraeth with a bold heart.
He was used to valleys. The shadow held him.
The staff and the fasces of tribunes betrayed him.
With the oil of our virtue we have anointed
His head, in the presence of foes.

Phillip Sweet of Cwmbach. Was he shy before girls?
He exposes himself now to the hags, the glance
Of the loose-fleshed whores, the deaths
That congregate like gulls on garbage.
His sword flashed in the wastes of nightmare.

Russell Carlisle of Rhuthun. Men of the North
Mourn Rheged's son in the castellated vale.
His nodding charger neighed for the battle.
Uplifted hooves pawed at the lightning.
Now he lies down. Under the air he is dead.

Men went to Catraeth. Of the forty-three
Certainly Tony Jones of Carmarthen was brave.
What did it matter, steel in the heart?
Shrapnel is faithful now. His shroud is frost.

With the dawn men went. Those forty-three,
Gentlemen all, from the streets and byways of Wales,
Dragons of Aberdare, Denbigh and Neath –
Figment of empire, whore's honour, held them.
Forty-three at Catraeth died for our dregs.

DAVID CONSTANTINE

Watching for Dolphins

In the summer months on every crossing to Piraeus
One noticed that certain passengers soon rose
From seats in the packed saloon and with serious
Looks and no acknowledgement of a common purpose
Passed forward through the small door into the bows
To watch for dolphins. One saw them lose

Every other wish. Even the lovers
Turned their desires on the sea, and a fat man
Hung with equipment to photograph the occasion
Stared like a saint, through sad bi-focals; others,
Hopeless themselves, looked to the children for they
Would see dolphins if anyone would. Day after day

Or on their last opportunity all gazed
Undecided whether a flat calm were favourable
Or a sea the sun and the wind between them raised
To a likeness of dolphins. Were gulls a sign, that fell
Screeching from the sky or over an unremarkable place
Sat in a silent school? Every face

After its character implored the sea.
All, unaccustomed, wanted epiphany,
Praying the sky would clang and the abused Aegean
Reverberate with cymbal, gong and drum.
We could not imagine more prayer, and had they then
On the waves, on the climax of our longing come

Smiling, snub-nosed, domed like satyrs, oh
We should have laughed and lifted the children up
Stranger to stranger, pointing how with a leap
They left their element, three or four times, centred
On grace, and heavily and warm re-entered,
Looping the keel. We should have felt them go

39

Further and further into the deep parts. But soon
We were among the great tankers, under their chains
In black water. We had not seen the dolphins
But woke, blinking. Eyes cast down
With no admission of disappointment the company
Dispersed and prepared to land in the city.

WENDY COPE

Engineers' Corner

Why isn't there an Engineers' Corner in Westminster Abbey?
In Britain we've always made more fuss of a ballad than a
blueprint . . . How many schoolchildren dream of becoming
great engineers?

Advertisement placed in The Times *by the*
Engineering Council

We make more fuss of ballads than of blueprints –
That's why so many poets end up rich,
While engineers scrape by in cheerless garrets.
Who needs a bridge or dam? Who needs a ditch?

Whereas the person who can write a sonnet
Has got it made. It's always been the way,
For everybody knows that we need poems
And everybody reads them every day.

Yes, life is hard if you choose engineering –
You're sure to need another job as well;
You'll have to plan your projects in the evenings
Instead of going out. It must be hell.

While well-heeled poets ride around in Daimlers,
You'll burn the midnight oil to earn a crust,
With no hope of a statue in the Abbey,
With no hope, even, of a modest bust.

No wonder small boys dream of writing couplets
And spurn the bike, the lorry and the train.
There's far too much encouragement for poets –
That's why this country's going down the drain.

KEVIN CROSSLEY-HOLLAND

Dusk, Burnham-Overy-Staithe

The blue hour ends, this world
floats on a great stillness.

I only guess where marsh
finishes and sky begins,

each grows out of the other.
In the creek a slip

of water gleams. Rowboats
bob and swing above the mud,

the barnacled and broken
ribs of Old Stoker's boat.

A wedge of gulls rustles
overhead, and for a moment

the water notices them.
Such calm is some prelude.

Then across the marsh it comes,
the sound as of an endless

train in a distant cutting,
the god working his way back,

butting and shunting,
reclaiming his territory.

The world's his soundbox now;
in the stillness he still moves.

Anything could happen.

TONY CURTIS

The Freezer

When they finally broke in
the place smelled like Pompeii –
dust, ash, fall-out inches thick.
She was sitting there, a queen propped
up in bed and not looking so hot.

In the garage an A.C.
road racer from the '30s worth thousands –
quality coachwork under the dust, and not a scratch.

All types of fungi in the kitchen
but the freezer was stocked and neat –
twenty-nine stiff cats packed and labelled:
'Roland' – 'Katherine' – 'Veronique' –
and so on, reading like a list of social
acquaintances. Curled, stretched, flat or sprung,
as if the shape gave each one a character.

The next evening, mackerel-eyed, fur
stuck like old pasting brushes,
they got shovelled into the garden.

The green eye of the freezer glowed,
the frosted chest purred and shuddered
in the empty house
until they cut off the mains.

Summer in Greece

Each day at noon the Englishman
drives into the sea.
He uses a seven-iron and places the balls
on a strip of carpet which he carries rolled
under his arm from the villa. A dozen
or two small splashes in the ocean.
They sink and cluster in the sand
gleaming like the hearts of opened sea-urchins.

Later, when it is cool, the boys swim out
and dive. They gather the balls—
Dunlop, Slazenger, Titleist, Penfold—
and return to the village. These are eggs
you can't crack or eat. They bounce.
There are no golf courses here.

Some mornings the Englishman from the villa
buys golf balls from the village.
They are cheap and the supply is constant.

DONALD DAVIE

Cherry Ripe

On a Painting by Juan Gris

No ripening curve can be allowed to sag
On cubist's canvas or in sculptor's stone:
Informal fruit, that burgeons from the swag,
Would spoil the ripening that is art's alone.

This can be done with cherries. Other fruit
Have too much bloom of import, like the grape,
Whose opulence comes welling from a root
Stuck far too deep to yield so pure a shape.

And Cherry ripe, indeed ripe, ripe, I cry.
Let orchards flourish in the poet's soul
And bear their feelings that are mastered by
Maturing rhythms, to compose a whole.

But how the shameful grapes and olives swell,
Excrescent from no cornucopia, tart,
Too near to oozing to be handled well:
Ripe, ripe, they cry, and perish in my heart.

The Fountain

Feathers up fast, and steeples; then in clods
Thuds into its first basin; thence as surf
Smokes up and hangs; irregularly slops
Into its second, tattered like a shawl;
There, chill as rain, stipples a danker green,
Where urgent tritons lob their heavy jets.

For Berkeley this was human thought, that mounts
From bland assumptions to inquiring skies,
There glints with wit, fumes into fancies, plays

With its negations, and at last descends,
As by a law of nature, to its bowl
Of thus enlightened but still common sense.

We who have no such confidence must gaze
With all the more affection on these forms,
These spires, these plumes, these calm reflections, these
Similitudes of surf and turf and shawl,
Graceful returns upon acceptances.
We ask of fountains only that they play,

Though that was not what Berkeley meant at all.

Put Not Your Trust in Princes

Let them give up the ghost, then there is nothing but
    dust
left of their presumptions we were fools enough to trust.

Pin no more hopes on them, nor the promissory
    collective;
the light at that end of the tunnel is glass, the credit
    delusive.

    In the presence of the authorities we spent our
        days
    turning our caps in our hands, and the manful,
        inveigling phrase.

    We combed our sparse hair in the mornings
        (silvered, we observed).
    We regarded our consort sleeping, whom we had
        shabbily served.

They are lost among the histories, names of world-
    mastering heroes:
this, the peace-fixer; that, the cuckolded smith of
    Infernos.

46

Having the sceptre no more, no more the ambiguous
    terms
of an unbelieved spokesman parade them; their press-
    men too feed worms.

CAROL ANN DUFFY

Standing Female Nude

Six hours like this for a few francs.
Belly nipple arse in the window light,
he drains the colour from me. Further to the right,
Madame. And do try to be still.
I shall be represented analytically and hung
in great museums. The bourgeoisie will coo
at such an image of a river-whore. They call it Art.

Maybe. He is concerned with volume, space.
I with the next meal. You're getting thin,
Madame, this is not good. My breasts hang
slightly low, the studio is cold. In the tea-leaves
I can see the Queen of England gazing
on my shape. Magnificent, she murmurs
moving on. It makes me laugh. His name

is Georges. They tell me he's a genius.
There are times he does not concentrate
and stiffens for my warmth. Men think of their mothers.
He possesses me on canvas as he dips the brush
repeatedly into the paint. Little man,
you've not the money for the arts I sell.
Both poor, we make our living how we can.

I ask him. Why do you do this? Because
I have to. There's no choice. Don't talk.
My smile confuses him. These artists
take themselves too seriously. At night I fill myself
with wine and dance around the bars. When it's
                                        finished
he shows me proudly, lights a cigarette. I say
Twelve francs and get my shawl. It does not look like
                                        me.

The Virgin Punishing the Infant

He spoke early. Not the *goo goo goo* of infancy,
but *I am God*. Joseph kept away, carving himself
a silent Pinocchio out in the workshed. He said
he was a simple man and hadn't dreamed of this.

She grew anxious in that second year, would stare
at stars saying *Gabriel? Gabriel?* Your guess.
The village gossiped in the sun. The child was solitary,
his wide and solemn eyes could fill your head.

After he walked, our normal children crawled. Our
                                        wives
were first resentful, then superior. Mary's child
would bring her sorrow . . . better far to have a son
who gurgled nonsense at your breast. *Googoo. Googoo.*

But I am God. We heard him through the window,
heard the smacks which made us peep. What we saw
was commonplace enough. But afterwards, we
                                   wondered
why the infant did not cry. And why the Mother did.

DOUGLAS DUNN

The Patricians

In small backyards old men's long underwear
Drips from sagging clotheslines.
The other stuff they take in bundles to the Bendix.

There chatty women slot their coins and joke
About the grey unmentionables absent.
The old men weaken in the steam and scratch at their
                                    rough chins.

Suppressing coughs and stiffnesses, they pedal bikes
On low gear slowly, in their faces
The effort to be upright, the dignity

That fits inside the smell of aromatic pipes.
Walking their dogs, the padded beats of pocket
                                    watches
Muffled under ancient overcoats, silences their hearts.

They live watching each other die, passing each other
In their white scarves, too long known to talk,
Waiting for the inheritance of the oldest, a right to
                                    power.

The street patricians, they are ignored.
Their anger proves something, their disenchantments
Settle round me like a cold fog.

They are the individualists of our time.
They know no fashions, copy nothing but their minds.
Long ago, they gave up looking in mirrors.

Dying in their sleep, they lie undiscovered.
The howling of their dogs brings the sniffing police,
Their middle-aged children from the new estates.

The Friendship of Young Poets

There must have been more than just one of us,
But we never met. Each kept in his world of loss
The promise of literary days, the friendship
Of poets, mysterious, that sharing of books
And talking in whispers in crowded bars
Suspicious enough to be taken for love.

We never met. My youth was as private
As the bank at midnight, and in its safety
No talking behind backs, no one alike enough
To be pretentious with and quote lines at.

There is a boat on the river now, and
Two young men, one rowing, one reading aloud.
Their shirt sleeves fill with wind, and from the oars
Drop scales of perfect river like melting glass.

Leaving Dundee

A small blue window opens in the sky
As thunder rumbles somewhere over Fife.
Eight months of up-and-down – goodbye, goodbye –
Since I sat listening to the wild geese cry
Fanatic flightpaths up autumnal Tay,
Instinctive, mad for home – make way! make way!
Communal feathered scissors, cutting through
The grievous artifice that was my life,
I was alert again, and listening to
That wavering, invisible V-dart
Between two bridges. Now, in a moistened puff,
Flags hang on the château-stacked gables of
A 1980s expense account hotel,
A lost French fantasy, baronial.
From here, through trees, its Frenchness hurts my
                                        heart.

It slips into a library of times.
Like an eye on a watch, it looks at me.
And I am going home on Saturday
To my house, to sit at my desk of rhymes
Among familiar things of love, that love me.
Down there, over the green and the railway yards,
Across the broad, rain-misted, subtle Tay,
The road home trickles to a house, a door.
She spoke of what I might do 'afterwards'.
'Go, somewhere else.' I went north to Dundee.
Tomorrow I won't live here any more,
Nor leave alone. *My love, say you'll come with me.*

A Snow-walk

What's haunting what, the birchwood or the snow?
It feels too European – this high, barbed fence,
A dog barking, a shot, and the sub-zero
Mid-winter rippled by a mortal cadence.

The water-tower near McGregor's house
Rejects its hurtful simile and slips
Behind the blizzard's curtain – ominous,
Re-memoried or rumoured guardianships.

White shelves on cypresses; and history's
Gaunt silver on a feathered crucifix –
A hawk nailed by its wings, a predatory
Snow-narrative retold in dead athletics.

Large tree-stumps, scattered through a chain-sawed
                                          wood,
Metamorphose to dust-cloth'd furniture,
Closed forest rooms, palatial solitude,
Iced armchairs and a branch-hung chandelier.

That fence again; a sign – *Guard Dogs Patrolling*.
Embedded in the snow, low huts appear,

A disused railway line, the shed for coaling,
A toppled goods van and a snow-filled brazier.

Home feels a life away and not an hour
Along the length of an industrial fence,
By friendly holdings and a water-tower
Robbed of simplicity and innocence.

D. J. ENRIGHT

Jingle Bells

Our presents were hidden on top of the cupboard.
Climbing up, we found a musical box, in the shape
Of a roller, which you pushed along the floor.

This was for our new sister, she was only
A few months old, her name was Valerie.

Just before Christmas (this I know is a memory
For no one ever spoke of it) the baby quietly
Disgorged a lot of blood, and was taken away.

The musical box disappeared too,
As my sister and I noted with mixed feelings.
We were not too old to play with it.

Master Kung at the Keyboard
(*for Lee Kum Sing*)

He's Oriental, he's Japanese, he's Chinese
Watch and you'll see him trip over his tail!
He's a child! What can he know of Vienna woods
Of Ludwig's deafness and J.S.B.'s fine ears?

Of tiaras and galas and programmes
Of hussars and cossacks and pogroms
Of Vespers, Valhallas and Wagrams
And the fine old flower of the Vienna woods?

(Wine, beef, pheasant, cheese, thirst, hunger)

Reared on rice and Taoist riddles
Water torture and the Yellow River
Yang Kwei-fei and one-stringed fiddles –
What can he know of the Water Music

Of barges and gondolas
Of emperors and haemophilias
Of the Abbé, the Princess, and her black cigars?

Wer das Dichten will verstehen
Muss ins Land der Dichtung gehen
Seven days with loaded Canon
Snapping prince and priest and peon.

So he went overseas for his studies? –
It is not in his blood.

What is in his blood?
Blood is.

(Rice, tea, pork, fish, hunger, thirst)

Compared with the minimum of 4,000 characters
Required at the finger-tips for near-literacy
And admission into provincial society
88 keys are child's play.

Play, child!

His heart pumps red rivers through his fingers
His hands chop Bechsteins into splinters
His breath ravishes the leaves
His hair never gets in his eyes.

I am down on my knees.

Every second pianist born is a Chinese
Schubert, Chopin, Mozart, Strauss and Liszt –
He'll be playing on
When the old Vienna woods have gone to chopsticks
Chopsticks every one.

Seaside Sensation

The strains of an elastic band
Waft softly o'er the sandy strand.
The maestro stretches out his hands
To bless the bandiest of bands.

Their instruments are big and heavy –
A glockenspiel for spieling Glock,
A handsome bandsome cuckoo clock
For use in Strauss (Johann not Lévi),

Deep-throated timpani in rows
For symphonies by Berlioz,
And lutes and flutes and concertinas,
Serpents, shawms and ocarinas.

The sun is shining, there are miles
Of peeling skin and healing smiles.
Also water which is doing
What it ought to, fro- and to-ing.

But can the band the bandstand stand?
Or can the bandstand stand the band?
The sand, the sand, it cannot stand
The strain of bandstand and a band!

Now swallowed up are band and stand
And smiling faces black and tanned.
The sand was quick and they were slow.
You hear them playing on below.

Abbey Going
(*i.m. Philip Larkin*)

Poets' Corner is somewhere to stand in,
In disgrace.
Giving the devil his due,
Your intellectual integrity – says the Sub-Dean
Up there at the holy end – denied you
The faith that could alone efface
Your lifelong fear of dying . . .
Some call it honest doubt.
Complaining we come in, and others complain
When we go out.

And then the psalm. 'I will take heed to my ways,
That I offend not in my tongue.
I will keep my mouth as it were with a bridle . . .'
You didn't publish very much. '. . . kept silence, yea,
But it was pain and grief to me.' (Also to us.)
But nor were you notably idle.
Followed by the Laureate reading the lesson
From the famous Ecclesiasticus,
And then – to the relief of many – Sidney Bechet.

As a send-off, somewhat curious!
They were playing at home, you were away.
How firm and frank the Church can be,
Inside a church.
Who is the less deceived is not for us to say.
You didn't especially love the garish day,
And now 'the night is gone'.
What it adds up to is, you couldn't lose.
You might as well have kept those bike-clips on.

RUTH FAINLIGHT

Animal Tamer

You would have made a good animal tamer –
I can tell by the way you're taming the wild black cat
that appeared last week at the bottom of the garden.
Every morning she comes a little further.
You go outside with a half-filled saucer of milk
and put it down as if you didn't care,
but each day move it an inch nearer the door.

The black cat's glaring eyes have a baffled look.
There's something about you she cannot understand.
You've activated her curiosity.
But still she crouches watchful under the bushes
until you glance away and fuss with your pipe,
and then she dashes across and gulps and laps,
the hair round her neck bristling with suspicion,
peering up at you several times a minute,
relieved yet puzzled by such indifference,
as though she missed the thrill of flight and escape.

Today, for the very first time, you turned and stared
at those yellow, survivor's eyes, and the cat stared back
a moment before she swerved and ran to safety.
But then she stopped, and doubled round and half
gave in, and soon, as I know well, you'll have
that cat, body pressed down on the earth and fur
electrified, stretching her limbs for mercy.

Introspection of a Sibyl

If only I could be aware of what is happening
in that void, that gap, that murky, fathomless cleft
where space and time must exist
between inspiration and the sound of my own voice:

the truth I never once have heard
a moment earlier than my listeners.

But I am no more conscious of the prophecies
than I can understand the language of birds.
A bird is singing now.
In spite of legend, like everyone else,
I wonder and guess at its message.
My oracles come like birdsong – or how I imagine
they must begin to sing – by instinct,
neither needing nor able to think.

The most terrible phrases burst from my mouth.
My profession is to doom strangers.
Already, as a girl,
playing ball with my friends in the village square
or feeding my tame pigeon, I remember
being more appalled than my parents
by what I'd say: an unforgivable insult
dealt out in all innocence, or a blurted sentence
like a gift to confirm good fortune.

How I admire control, and yearn to achieve it.
I've become almost grateful to those who control me.
Before, I never knew when it would begin.
But the closed, startled expressions
on the faces of those standing round
– as though shutters crashed down –
meant again I'd defined or foretold,
unerringly exposed the poor secret
some old man kept hidden all his life:

with sight as sharp as an eagle
who spots the frightened creature
veering back and forth, exhausted,
across a rocky mountainside,
maddened by the shadow of its wings –
and heavier than every element,
surer than the laws of gravity,

swoops for the kill.

After a few times, you recognize
a universal wariness. It takes longer
to fear yourself, to accept the certainty
of never illuminating that blankness,
the vital hiatus when the demon or angel,
the god, perhaps, takes possession
and you don't exist
yet have the power of a god.

Panic of falling – said to be
the sole inborn fear of a human infant.
Deeper than fear, I've learned, lies the greatest pleasure:
nausea and exhilaration of plummeting free,
the glee of surrender to nullity, temptation
more primal than any craving for security.

And the price for such knowledge? To have
absolutely no command over your life,
your words – no possibility
of calculated effects or tactics or policy.
But how useful you can be to others; and how lucky
if rather than burning or stoning, they protect you,
feed you, and let the simple folk praise you,
keep you safe as a caged bird,
and call you a sibyl.

U. A. FANTHORPE

Not My Best Side

(*Uccello:* S. George and the Dragon, *The National Gallery*)

I
Not my best side, I'm afraid.
The artist didn't give me a chance to
Pose properly, and as you can see,
Poor chap, he had this obsession with
Triangles, so he left off two of my
Feet. I didn't comment at the time
(What, after all, are two feet
To a monster?) but afterwards
I was sorry for the bad publicity.
Why, I said to myself, should my conqueror
Be so ostentatiously beardless, and ride
A horse with a deformed neck and square hoofs?
Why should my victim be so
Unattractive as to be inedible,
And why should she have me literally
On a string? I don't mind dying
Ritually, since I always rise again,
But I should have liked a little more blood
To show they were taking me seriously.

II
It's hard for a girl to be sure if
She wants to be rescued. I mean, I quite
Took to the dragon. It's nice to be
Liked, if you know what I mean. He was
So nicely physical, with his claws
And lovely green skin, and that sexy tail,
And the way he looked at me,
He made me feel he was all ready to
Eat me. And any girl enjoys that.
So when this boy turned up, wearing machinery,
On a really *dangerous* horse, to be honest,

61

I didn't much fancy him. I mean,
What was he like underneath the hardware?
He might have acne, blackheads or even
Bad breath for all I could tell, but the dragon –
Well, you could see all his equipment
At a glance. Still, what could I do?
The dragon got himself beaten by the boy,
And a girl's got to think of her future.

III
I have diplomas in Dragon
Management and Virgin Reclamation.
My horse is the latest model, with
Automatic transmission and built-in
Obsolescence. My spear is custom-built,
And my prototype armour
Still on the secret list. You can't
Do better than me at the moment.
I'm qualified and equipped to the
Eyebrow. So why be difficult?
Don't you want to be killed and/or rescued
In the most contemporary way? Don't
You want to carry out the roles
That sociology and myth have designed for you?
Don't you realize that, by being choosy,
You are endangering job-prospects
In the spear- and horse-building industries?
What, in any case, does it matter what
You want? You're in my way.

Rising Damp
(for C. A. K. and R. K. M.)

'A river can sometimes be diverted, but it is a very hard thing
to lose it altogether.'
    J. G. Head, paper read to the Auctioneers' Institute in 1907

At our feet they lie low,
The little fervent underground
Rivers of London

Effra, Graveney, Falcon, Quaggy,
Wandle, Walbrook, Tyburn, Fleet

Whose names are disfigured,
Frayed, effaced.

These are the Magogs that chewed the clay
To the basin that London nestles in.
These are the currents that chiselled the city,
That washed the clothes and turned the mills,
Where children drank and salmon swam
And wells were holy.

They have gone under.
Boxed, like the magician's assistant.
Buried alive in earth.
Forgotten, like the dead.

They return spectrally after heavy rain,
Confounding suburban gardens. They infiltrate
Chronic bronchitis statistics. A silken
Slur haunts dwellings by shrouded
Watercourses, and is taken
For the footing of the dead.

Being of our world, they will return
(Westbourne, caged at Sloane Square,
Will jack from his box),
Will deluge cellars, detonate manholes,
Plant effluent on our faces,
Sink the city.

Effra, Graveney, Falcon, Quaggy,
Wandle, Walbrook, Tyburn, Fleet

It is the other rivers that lie
Lower, that touch us only in dreams
That never surface. We feel their tug
As a dowser's rod bends to the source below

Phlegethon, Acheron, Lethe, Styx.

'Soothing and Awful'

(Visitors' Book at Montacute church)

You are meant to exclaim. The church
Expects it of you. Bedding plants
And polished brass anticipate a word.

Visitors jot a name,
A nationality, briskly enough,
But find *Remarks* beyond them.

I love English churches!
Says Friedrichshafen expansively.
The English are more backward. They come,

Certainly, from Spalding, Westbury-on-Trym,
The Isle of Wight; but all the words
They know are: *Very Lovely; Very Peaceful; Nice.*

A giggling gaggle from Torquay Grammar,
All pretending they can't spell *beautiful,* concoct
A private joke about the invisible organ.

A civilized voice from Cambridge
Especially noticed the well-kept churchyard.
Someone from Dudley, whose writing suggests tight
                                        shoes,

Reported *Nice and Cool.* The young entry
Yelp their staccato approval:
Super! Fantastic! Jesus Lives! Ace!

But what they found,
Whatever it was, it wasn't what
They say. In the beginning,

We know, the word, but not here,
Land of the perpetually-flowering cliché,
The rigid lip. Our fathers who piled

Stone upon stone, our mothers
Who stitched the hassocks, our cousins
Whose bones lie smooth, harmonious around –

However majestic their gifts, comely their living,
Their words would be thin like ours; they would join
In our inarticulate anthem: *Very Cosy*.

ELAINE FEINSTEIN

Anniversary

Suppose I took out a slender ketch from
under the spokes of Palace pier tonight to
catch a sea-going fish for you

or dressed in antique goggles and wings and
flew down through sycamore leaves into the park

or luminescent through some planetary strike
put one delicate flamingo leg over the sill of your lab

Could I surprise you? or would you insist on
keeping a pattern to link every transfiguration?

Listen, I shall have to whisper it
into your heart directly: we are all
supernatural / every day
we rise new creatures / cannot be predicted

Mother love

You eat me, your
nights eat me
Once you took
haemoglobin and bone
out of my blood

Now my head
sleeps forward on my neck
holding you

In the morning my
skin shines hot
and you are happy
banging your fat hands

I kiss your
soft feet mindless:
delicately

your shit slides out
yellow and
smelling of curd cheese.

In a Notebook

There was a river overhung with trees
With wooden houses built along its shallows
From which the morning sun drew up a haze
And the gyrations of the early swallows
Paid no attention to the gentle breeze
Which spoke discreetly from the weeping willows.
There was a jetty by the forest clearing
Where a small boat was tugging at its mooring.

And night still lingered underneath the eaves.
In the dark houseboats families were stirring
And Chinese soup was cooked on charcoal stoves.
Then one by one there came into the clearing
Mothers and daughters bowed beneath their sheaves.
The silent children gathered round me staring
And the shy soldiers setting out for battle
Asked for a cigarette and laughed a little.

From low canoes old men laid out their nets
While on the bank young boys with lines were fishing.
The wicker traps were drawn up by their floats.
The girls stood waist-deep in the river washing
Or tossed the day's rice on enamel plates
And I sat drinking bitter coffee wishing
The tide would turn to bring me to my senses
After the pleasant war and the evasive answers.

There was a river overhung with trees.
The girls stood waist-deep in the river washing,
And night still lingered underneath the eaves
While on the bank young boys with lines were fishing.
Mothers and daughters bowed beneath their sheaves
While I sat drinking bitter coffee wishing –
And the tide turned and brought me to my senses.
The pleasant war brought the unpleasant answers.

The villages are burnt, the cities void;
The morning light has left the river view;
The distant followers have been dismayed;
And I'm afraid, reading this passage now,
That everything I knew has been destroyed
By those whom I admired but never knew;
The laughing soldiers fought to their defeat
And I'm afraid most of my friends are dead.

ROY FISHER

Toyland

Today the sunlight is the paint on lead soldiers
Only they are people scattering out of the cool church

And as they go across the gravel and among the spring
                    streets
They spread formality: they know, we know, what they
                    have been doing,

The old couples, the widowed, the staunch smilers,
The deprived and the few nubile young lily-ladies,

And we know what they will do when they have
                    opened the doors of their houses
                    and walked in:
Mostly they will make water, and wash their calm hands
                    and eat.

The organ's flourishes finish; the verger closes the
                    doors;
The choirboys run home, and the rector goes off in his
                    motor.

Here a policeman stalks, the sun glinting on his helmet-
                    crest;
Then a man pushes a perambulator home; and
                    somebody posts a letter.

If I sit here long enough, loving it all, I shall see the
                    District Nurse pedal past,
The children going to Sunday School and the strollers
                    strolling;

The lights darting on in different rooms as night comes
                                in;
And I shall see washing hung out, and the postman
                    delivering letters.

I might by exception see an ambulance or the fire
                            brigade
Or even, if the chance came round, street musicians
                    (singing and playing).

For the people I've seen, this seems the operation of
                            life:
I need the paint of stillness and sunshine to see it that
                    way.

The secret laugh of the world picks them up and shakes
                    them like peas boiling;
They behave as if nothing happened; maybe they no
                    longer notice.

I notice. I laugh with the laugh, cultivate it, make much
                            of it,
But I still don't know what the joke is, to tell them.

Paraphrases
(for Peter Ryan)

Dear Mr Fisher I am writing
a thesis on your work.
But am unable to obtain
texts. I have articles by Davie, D.,
and Mottram, E.,
but not your Books since booksellers
I have approached refuse to
take my order saying they

can no longer afford to
handle 'this type of business'. It is
too late! for me to change
my subject to the work of a more
popular writer, so please Mr Fisher
you must help me since I face the alternatives
of failing my degree or repaying
the whole of my scholarship money . . .

Dear Mr Fisher although I have been unable
to read much of your work (to get it that is)
I am a great admirer of it and your landscapes
have become so real to me I am convinced I have, in
                    fact,
become you. I have never, however,
seen any photograph of you, and am most curious
to have an idea of your appearance,
beyond what my mirror, of course, tells me.
The cover of your *Collected Poems*
(reproduced in the *Guardian*, November 1971)
shows upwards of fifty faces; but which is yours? Are
            you
the little boy at the front, and if so have you
changed much since then?

Dear Mr Fisher recently while studying
selections from a modern anthology with
one of my GCE groups I came across your interestingly
            titled
'Starting to Make a Tree'. After the discussion I felt
            strongly
you were definitely *holding something back* in this poem
though I can't quite reach it. Are you often in Rugby?
If you are, perhaps we could meet and I could
try at least to explain. Cordially, Avis Tree. PS. Should
            we
arrange a rendezvous I'm afraid I wouldn't
know who to look out for as I've never unfortunately

seen your photograph. But I notice you were born in
        1930
the same year as Ted Hughes. Would I be right
in expecting you to resemble *him*, more or less?

                              – Dear Ms Tree,
It's true I'm in Rugby quite often, but the train
goes through without stopping. Could you fancy
        standing
outside the UP Refreshment Room a few times so that
I could learn to recognize *you*? If you could
just get hold of my four books, and wave them,
then I'd know it was you. As for my own appearance
I suppose it inclines more to the
Philip Larkin side of Ted Hughes's looks . . .
So if you think so as I go by . . .

Dear Mr Fisher I have been commissioned
to write a short
critical book on your work
but find that although I have a full
dossier of reviews etcetera
I don't have access to your books. Libraries
over here seem just not to have bought them in.
Since the books are quite a few years old now
I imagine they'll all have been remaindered
some while back? Or worse, pulped? So can
you advise me on locating second-hand copies,
not too expensively I hope? Anyway,
yours, with apologies and respect . . .

Dear Mr Fisher I am now
so certain I am you that it is obvious to me
that the collection of poems I am currently working on
        must be
your own next book! Can you let me know –
who is to publish it and exactly when
it will be appearing? I shouldn't like there to

be any trouble over contracts, 'plagiarism'
etcetera; besides which it would be a pity
to think one of us was wasting time and effort.
How far have *you* got? Please help me. I
do think this is urgent . . .

A Sign Illuminated

In honour of something or other –
King Bertie's crowning; the Charter Centenary;
1938 as a whole – the city

decreed that on several occasions there should emerge
from the Depot on Kyotts Lake Road an Illuminated
Bus. On a published route

it would slowly glide through every
suburb and slum in turn. Crowds
might turn out. So it came

cruising on summer evenings, before
the little boys went to their beds, its lights
plain in the sun from as much as a mile off;

those lights were its headlamps and certain thin
patterns of domestic bulbs
all over the coachwork. What the city had picked

was one of its own
retired double-deckers. They'd sliced off the top,
blacked the windows, painted out the livery;

it was a vehicle so old
that the shadowy driver sat exposed above the engine
in an open cab. Among the little boys

were many who knew the design and the period
registration plates. In the sunset light
they could take it all in: this emblem

that trundled past all the stops; possessed no
route number, passengers or conductor; was less than
a bus, let alone less than lit up.

JOHN FULLER

Daughter

Once inside my head
The thought is hard to get out:
   Another daughter.

You were never ours.
Photographs showed you missing
   And no one noticed.

Intention was blind:
How near was your conception
   We shall never know.

The disqualified
Candidates can't believe the
   Office is unfilled.

You don't exist, but
Nobody can take your place:
   That space has been booked.

Three faces suggest
The fourth: compass points of the
   Parental axes.

Words like little loves
Presiding over a map
   For future journeys.

Prospero's secret
Sadness: I had peopled else
   This isle with daughters.

Only the subject
Of unuseful poetry:
What never occurred.

Concerto for Double Bass

He is a drunk leaning companionably
Around a lamp post or doing up
With intermittent concentration
Another drunk's coat.

He is a polite but devoted Valentino,
Cheek to cheek, forgetting the next step.
He is feeling the pulse of the fat lady
Or cutting her in half.

But close your eyes and it is sunset
At the edge of the world. It is the language
Of dolphins, the growth of tree-roots,
The heart-beat slowing down.

Valentine

The things about you I appreciate
        May seem indelicate:
I'd like to find you in the shower
And chase the soap for half an hour.
I'd like to have you in my power
        And see your eyes dilate.
I'd like to have your back to scour
And other parts to lubricate.
Sometimes I feel it is my fate
To chase you screaming up a tower
        Or make you cower
By asking you to differentiate
        Nietzsche from Schopenhauer.
I'd like successfully to guess your weight
        And win you at a fête.
I'd like to offer you a flower.

I like the hair upon your shoulders,
Falling like water over boulders.
I like the shoulders, too: they are essential.
Your collar-bones have great potential
(I'd like all your particulars in folders
    Marked *Confidential*).

I like your cheeks, I like your nose,
I like the way your lips disclose
The neat arrangement of your teeth
(Half above and half beneath)
    In rows.

I like your eyes, I like their fringes.
The way they focus on me gives me twinges.
Your upper arms drive me berserk.
I like the way your elbows work,
    On hinges.

I like your wrists, I like your glands,
I like the fingers on your hands.
I'd like to teach them how to count,
And certain things we might exchange,
Something familiar for something strange.
I'd like to give you just the right amount
    And get some change.

I like it when you tilt your cheek up.
I like the way you nod and hold a teacup.
I like your legs when you unwind them.
Even in trousers I don't mind them.
I like each softly-moulded kneecap.
I like the little crease behind them.
I'd always know, without a recap,
    Where to find them.

I like the sculpture of your ears.
I like the way your profile disappears
Whenever you decide to turn and face me.

I'd like to cross two hemispheres
    And have you chase me.
I'd like to smuggle you across frontiers
Or sail with you at night into Tangiers.
    I'd like you to embrace me.

I'd like to see you ironing your skirt
    And cancelling other dates.
I'd like to button up your shirt.
I like the way your chest inflates.
I'd like to soothe you when you're hurt
Or frightened senseless by invertebrates.

I'd like you even if you were malign
And had a yen for sudden homicide.
I'd let you put insecticide
    Into my wine.
I'd even like you if you were the Bride
    Of Frankenstein
Or something ghoulish out of Mamoulian's
    Jekyll and Hyde.
I'd even like you as my Julian
Of Norwich or Cathleen ni Houlihan.
    How melodramatic
If you were something muttering in attics
Like Mrs Rochester or a student of Boolean
    Mathematics.

You are the end of self-abuse.
You are the eternal feminine.
I'd like to find a good excuse
To call on you and find you in.
I'd like to put my hand beneath your chin,
    And see you grin.
I'd like to taste your Charlotte Russe,
I'd like to feel my lips upon your skin,
I'd like to make you reproduce.

I'd like you in my confidence.
I'd like to be your second look.
I'd like to let you try the French Defence
    And mate you with my rook.
I'd like to be your preference
    And hence
I'd like to be around when you unhook.
I'd like to be your only audience,
The final name in your appointment book,
    Your future tense.

VALERIE GILLIES

The Piano Tuner

Two hundred miles, he had come
    to tune one piano, the last hereabouts.
Both of them were relics of imperial time:
    the Anglo-Indian and the old upright knock-about.

He peered, and peered again
    into its monsoon-warped bowels.
From the flats of dead sound he'd beckon
    a tune on the bones out to damp vowels.

His own sounds were pidgin.
    The shapeliness of his forearms
lent his body an English configuration,
    but still, sallow as any snakecharmer

he was altogether piebald.
    Far down the bridge of his nose
perched roundrimmed tortoiseshell spectacles;
    his hair, a salt-and-pepper, white foreclosed.

But he rings in the ear yet,
    his interminable tapping of jarring notes:
and, before he left,
    he gave point to those hours of discord.

With a smile heavenly
    because so out of place, cut off from any home
                                there,
he sat down quietly
    to play soft music: that tune of 'Beautiful Dreamer',

a melody seized from yellowed ivories
    and rotting wood. A damper
muffled the pedal point of lost birthright. We eaves-
    dropped on an extinct creature.

PHILIP GROSS

Son and Heir

He's up. And off, a tipsy
   tightrope turn
juggling with gravity.
   The ascent of man
starts here. Like one spotlit

   he makes his stand
on the brink of a big-top
   drop. The ground
sways. One false step
   and . . .

Will he take it stonily
   like Sitting Bull?
Like holy Job? Or melancholy
   Charlie, fall-
guy to the old joke? Will he

   heck! He's baby-bald
Khrushchev, blamming a shoe
   on the diplomatic table –
'WE WILL BURY YOU . . .'

   No joke. He will.

From the Fast Train

The town falls by the wayside. Gone astray
in the urban outback, our racketing dulls
to an auctioneer's gabble. Rails splay
into rusty shuntings. Long grass rankles.
There's a rash of fireweed, smatterings of may

and there, gone feral on clinker, a shock
of lupins, wild colonials. Was that a goat
cropping the scrub beside a landlocked
quarter acre? Scratched earth and a rain-butt?
Thin smoke tippling from a corrugated shack

no path leads to or from? And who'd
be waiting there, who'd be at home
nursing a Coronation mug, tea stewed
to a metallic tang? Yes, that's him.
'Such a time,' he'd say 'What kept you?'

THOM GUNN

Vox Humana

Being without quality
I appear to you at first
as an unkempt smudge, a blur,
an indefinite haze, mere-
ly pricking the eyes, almost
nothing. Yet you perceive me.

I have been always most close
when you had least resistance,
falling asleep, or in bars;
during the unscheduled hours,
though strangely without substance,
I hang, there and ominous.

Aha, sooner or later
you will have to name me, and,
as you name, I shall focus,
I shall become more precise.
O Master (for you command
in naming me, you prefer)!

I was, for Alexander,
the certain victory; I
was hemlock for Socrates;
and, in the dry night, Brutus
waking before Philippi
stopped me, crying out, 'Caesar!'

Or if you call me the blur
that in fact I am, you shall
yourself remain blurred, hanging
like smoke indoors. For you bring,
to what you define now, all
there is, ever, of future.

From the Wave

It mounts at sea, a concave wall
   Down-ribbed with shine,
And pushes forward, building tall
   Its steep incline.

Then from their hiding rise to sight
   Black shapes on boards
Bearing before the fringe of white
   It mottles towards.

Their pale feet curl, they poise their weight
   With a learn'd skill.
It is the wave they imitate
   Keeps them so still.

The marbling bodies have become
   Half wave, half men,
Grafted it seems by feet of foam
   Some seconds, then,

Late as they can, they slice the face
   In timed procession:
Balance is triumph in this place,
   Triumph possession.

The mindless heave of which they rode
   A fluid shelf
Breaks as they leave it, falls and, slowed,
   Loses itself.

Clear, the sheathed bodies slick as seals
   Loosen and tingle;
And by the board the bare foot feels
   The suck of shingle.

They paddle in the shallows still;
    Two splash each other;
Then all swim out to wait until
    The right waves gather.

Yoko

All today I lie in the bottom of the wardrobe
feeling low but sometimes getting up
to moodily lumber across rooms
and lap from the toilet bowl, it is so sultry
and then I hear the noise of firecrackers again
all New York is jaggedy with firecrackers today
and I go back to the wardrobe gloomy
trying to void my mind of them.
I am confused, I feel loose and unfitted.

At last deep in the stairwell I hear a tread,
it is him, my leader, my love.
I run to the door and listen to his approach.
Now I can smell him, what a good man he is,
I love it when he has the sweat of work on him,
as he enters I yodel with happiness,
I throw my body up against his, I try to lick his lips,
I care about him more than anything.

After we eat we go for a walk to the piers.
I leap into the standing warmth, I plunge into
the combination of old and new smells.
Here on a garbage can at the bottom, so interesting,
what sister or brother I wonder left this message I sniff.
I too piss there, and go on.
Here a hydrant there a pole
here's a smell I left yesterday, well that's disappointing
but I piss there anyway, and go on.
I investigate so much that in the end
it is for form's sake only, only a drop comes out.

86

I investigate tar and rotten sandwiches, everything, and
                                        go on.

And here a dried old turd, so interesting
so old, so dry, yet so subtle and mellow.
I can place it finely, I really appreciate it,
a gold distant smell like packed autumn leaves in winter
reminding me how what is rich and fierce when
                                excreted
becomes weathered and mild
                        but always interesting
and reminding me of what I have to do.

My leader looks on and expresses his approval.

I sniff it well and later I sniff the air well
a wind is meeting us after the close July day
rain is getting near too but first the wind.

Joy, joy,
being outside with you, active, investigating it all,
with bowels emptied, feeling your approval
and then running on, the big fleet Yoko,
my body in its excellent black coat never lets me down,
returning to you (as I always will, you know that)
and now
            filling myself out with myself, no longer
                                confused,
my panting pushing apart my black lips, but unmoving,
I stand with you braced against the wind.

Hide and Seek

Children play on into
the summer evening, the block
full of excited shouts.
These girls tied a rope
to the lamp post higher and higher.
Others sing slightly off-key

counting-out songs, and songs
from TV and Sunday school.
Across the street
                    boys and girls
whoosh by on skate boards
that rumble to the end of the block.

From trees behind the houses
birds are calling
about the gathering night.
Chicks scramble
among the familiar ordure
loose-clotted in the nest.

In their fathers' gardens
children are hiding
up in orchard trees, seeking
to be lost and found.

Mother comes down
for the youngest
and as the dark thickens
for the oldest too.

Indoors, under a naked bulb,
eight puppies sleep
close against the huge hairy body
of their mother. The bees
have returned to their Queen.
The crescent moon rises
nine-tenths of it still hidden
but imperceptibly moving
below the moving stars
and hugging the earth.

MICHAEL HAMBURGER

A Poet's Progress

Like snooker balls thrown on the table's faded green,
Rare ivory and weighted with his best ambitions,
At first his words are launched: not certain what they
                                   mean,
He loves to see them roll, rebound, assume positions
Which – since not he – some higher power has assigned.
But now the game begins: dead players, living critics
Are watching him – and suddenly one eye goes blind,
The hand that holds the cue shakes like a paralytic's,
Till every thudding, every clinking sound portends
New failure, new defeat. Amazed, he finds that still
It is not he who guides his missiles to their ends
But an unkind geometry that mocks his will.

If he persists, for years he'll practise patiently,
Lock all the doors, learn all the tricks, keep noises out,
Though he may pick a ghost or two for company
Or pierce the room's inhuman silence with a shout.
More often silence wins; then soon the green felt seems
An evil playground, lawless, lost to time, forsaken,
And he a fool caught in the water weeds of dreams
Whom only death or frantic effort can awaken.

At last, a master player, he can face applause,
Looks for a fit opponent, former friends, emerges;
But no one knows him now. He questions his own
                                   cause
And has forgotten why he yielded to those urges,
Took up a wooden cue to strike a coloured ball.
Wise now, he goes on playing; both his house and heart
Unguarded solitudes, hospitable to all
Who can endure the cold intensity of art.

Solidarity

There's honour among thieves, both in and out of
                                    prison
Fellowship even, in the teeth of competition,
And sorority among whores – though mainly off-duty,
On sea-side vacations, or after the ruin of beauty –
But strongest and strangest of all is the solidarity
Of respectable men in respectable company.
Would it be drink that does it? Dissolving differences,
Discrete achievements and individual purities?
No, they feel it when sober, not only at parties and
                                    luncheons
But in boardrooms, common rooms, barracks, or
                    charging with truncheons.
It comes over them suddenly – not a warm, not a vernal
                                    breath,
Yet kindling warmth in cold hearts – the bad conscience
                                    of death,
Communist at the frontier bound in time to break
                            through,
But, teacher of love among convicts, Christian too.

TONY HARRISON

Them & [uz]
(*for Professors Richard Hoggart & Leon Cortez*)

I

αἰαῖ, ay, ay! . . . stutterer Demosthenes
gob full of pebbles outshouting seas –

4 words only of *mi 'art aches* and . . . 'Mine's broken,
you barbarian, T.W.!' *He* was nicely spoken.
'Can't have our glorious heritage done to death!'

I played the Drunken Porter in *Macbeth*.

'Poetry's the speech of kings. You're one of those
Shakespeare gives the comic bits to: prose!
All poetry (even Cockney Keats?) you see
's been dubbed by [ʌs] into RP,
Received Pronunciation, please believe [ʌs]
your speech is in the hands of the Receivers.'

'We say [ʌs] not [uz] T.W.!' That shut my trap.
I doffed my flat a's (as in 'flat cap')
my mouth all stuffed with glottals, great
lumps to hawk up and spit out . . . *E-nun-ci-ate*!

II

So right, yer buggers, then! We'll occupy
your lousy leasehold Poetry.

I chewed up Littererchewer and spat the bones
into the lap of dozing Daniel Jones,
dropped the initials I'd been harried as
and used my *name* and own voice: [uz] [uz] [uz],
ended sentences with by, with, from,

and spoke the language that I spoke at home.
R.I.P. RP, R.I.P. T.W.
I'm *Tony* Harrison no longer you!

You can tell the Receivers where to go
(and not aspirate it) once you know
Wordsworth's *matter/water* are full rhymes,
[uz] can be loving as well as funny.

My first mention in the *Times*
automatically made Tony Anthony!

Book Ends[1]

Baked the day she suddenly dropped dead
we chew it slowly that last apple pie.

Shocked into sleeplessness you're scared of bed.
We never could talk much, and now don't try.

You're like book ends, the pair of you, she'd say,
Hog that grate, say nothing, sit, sleep, stare . . .

The 'scholar' me, you, worn out on poor pay,
only our silence made us seem a pair.

Not as good for staring in, blue gas,
too regular each bud, each yellow spike.

A night you need my company to pass
and she not here to tell us we're alike!

Your life's all shattered into smithereens.

Back in our silences and sullen looks,
for all the Scotch we drink, what's still between 's
not the thirty or so years, but books, books, books.

Long Distance 2

Though my mother was already two years dead
Dad kept her slippers warming by the gas,
put hot water bottles her side of the bed
and still went to renew her transport pass.

You couldn't just drop in. You had to phone.
He'd put you off an hour to give him time
to clear away her things and look alone
as though his still raw love were such a crime.

He couldn't risk my blight of disbelief
though sure that very soon he'd hear her key
scrape in the rusted lock and end his grief.
He *knew* she'd just popped out to get the tea.

I believe life ends with death, and that is all.
You haven't both gone shopping; just the same,
in my new black leather phone book there's your name
and the disconnected number I still call.

SEAMUS HEANEY

The Outlaw

Kelly's kept an unlicensed bull, well away
From the road: you risked fine but had to pay

The normal fee if cows were serviced there.
Once I dragged a nervous Friesian on a tether

Down a lane of alder, shaggy with catkin,
Down to the shed the bull was kept in.

I gave Old Kelly the clammy silver, though why
I could not guess. He grunted a curt 'Go by

Get up on that gate.' And from my lofty station
I watched the business-like conception.

The door, unbolted, whacked back against the wall.
The illegal sire fumbled from his stall

Unhurried as an old steam engine shunting.
He circled, snored and nosed. No hectic panting,

Just the unfussy ease of a good tradesman;
Then an awkward, unexpected jump, and

His knobbled forelegs straddling her flank,
He slammed life home, impassive as a tank,

Dropping off like a tipped-up load of sand.
'She'll do,' said Kelly and tapped his ash-plant

Across her hindquarters. 'If not, bring her back.'
I walked ahead of her, the rope now slack

While Kelly whooped and prodded his outlaw
Who, in his own time, resumed the dark, the straw.

The Skunk

Up, black, striped and damasked like the chasuble
At a funeral mass, the skunk's tail
Paraded the skunk. Night after night
I expected her like a visitor.

The refrigerator whinnied into silence.
My desk light softened beyond the verandah.
Small oranges loomed in the orange tree.
I began to be tense as a voyeur.

After eleven years I was composing
Love-letters again, broaching the word 'wife'
Like a stored cask, as if its slender vowel
Had mutated into the night earth and air

Of California. The beautiful, useless
Tang of eucalyptus spelt your absence.
The aftermath of a mouthful of wine
Was like inhaling you off a cold pillow.

And there she was, the intent and glamorous,
Ordinary, mysterious skunk,
Mythologized, demythologized,
Snuffing the boards five feet beyond me.

It all came back to me last night, stirred
By the sootfall of your things at bedtime,
Your head-down, tail-up hunt in a bottom drawer
For the black plunge-line nightdress.

Punishment

I can feel the tug
of the halter at the nape
of her neck, the wind
on her naked front.

It blows her nipples
to amber beads,
it shakes the frail rigging
of her ribs.

I can see her drowned
body in the bog,
the weighing stone,
the floating rods and boughs.

Under which at first
she was a barked sapling
that is dug up
oak-bone, brain-firkin:

her shaved head
like a stubble of black corn,
her blindfold a soiled bandage,
her noose a ring

to store
the memories of love.
Little adulteress,
before they punished you

you were flaxen-haired,
undernourished, and your
tar-black face was beautiful.
My poor scapegoat,

I almost love you
but would have cast, I know,

the stones of silence.
I am the artful voyeur

of your brain's exposed
and darkened combs,
your muscles' webbing
and all your numbered bones:

I who have stood dumb
when your betraying sisters,
cauled in tar,
wept by the railings,

who would connive
in civilized outrage
yet understand the exact
and tribal, intimate revenge.

From Clearances

3

When all the other were away at Mass
I was all hers as we peeled potatoes.
They broke the silence, let fall one by one
Like solder weeping off the soldering iron:
Cold comforts set between us, things to share
Gleaming in a bucket of clean water.
And again let fall. Little pleasant splashes
From each other's work would bring us to our senses.

So while the parish priest at her bedside
Went hammer and tongs at the prayers for the dying
And some were responding and some crying
I remembered her head bent towards my head,
Her breath in mine, our fluent dipping knives –
Never closer the whole rest of our lives.

GEOFFREY HILL

From Funeral Music
3

They bespoke doomsday and they meant it by
God, their curved metal rimming the low ridge.
But few appearances are like this. Once
Every five hundred years a comet's
Over-riding stillness might reveal men
In such array, livid and featureless,
With England crouched beastwise beneath it all.
'Oh, that old northern business . . .' A field
After battle utters its own sound
Which is like nothing on earth, but is earth.
Blindly the questing snail, vulnerable
Mole emerge, blindly we lie down, blindly
Among carnage the most delicate souls
Tup in their marriage-blood, gasping 'Jesus'.

7

'Prowess, vanity, mutual regard,
It seemed I stared at them, they at me.
That was the gorgon's true and mortal gaze:
Averted conscience turned against itself.'
A hawk and a hawk-shadow. 'At noon,
As the armies met, each mirrored the other;
Neither was outshone. So they flashed and vanished
And all that survived them was the stark ground
Of this pain. I made no sound, but once
I stiffened as though a remote cry
Had heralded my name. It was nothing . . .'
Reddish ice tinged the reeds; dislodged, a few
Feathers drifted across; carrion birds
Strutted upon the armour of the dead.

Merlin

I will consider the outnumbering dead:
For they are the husks of what was rich seed.
Now, should they come together to be fed,
They would outstrip the locusts' covering tide.

Arthur, Elaine, Mordred; they are all gone
Among the raftered galleries of bone.
By the long barrows of Logres they are made one,
And over their city stands the pinnacled corn.

Idylls of the King

The pigeon purrs in the wood; the wood has gone;
dark leaves that flick to silver in the gust,
and the marsh-orchids and the heron's nest,
goldgrimy shafts and pillars of the sun.

Weightless magnificence upholds the past.
Cement recesses smell of fur and bone
and berries wrinkle in the badger-run
and wiry heath-fern scatters its fresh rust.

'O clap your hands' so that the dove takes flight,
bursts through the leaves with an untidy sound,
plunges its wings into the green twilight

above this long-sought and forsaken ground,
the half-built ruins of the new estate,
warheads of mushrooms round the filter-pond.

MICHAEL HOFMANN

Ancient Evenings
(for A.)

My friends hunted in packs, had themselves
                                photographed
under hoardings that said 'Tender Vegetables'
or 'Big Chunks', but I had you – my Antonia!
Not for long, nor for a long time now . . .

Later, your jeans faded more completely,
and the hole in them wore to a furred square,
as it had to, but I remember my hands
skating over them, there where the cloth was thickest.

You were so quiet, it seemed like an invitation
to be disturbed, like Archimedes and the soldier,
like me, like the water displaced from my kettle
when I heated tins of viscous celery soup in it

until the glue dissolved and the labels crumbled
and the turbid, overheated water turned into more
                                soup . . .
I was overheated, too. I could not trust my judgement.
The coffee I made in the dark was eight times too strong.

My humour was gravity, so I sat us both in an armchair
and toppled over backwards. I must have hoped
the experience of danger would cement our
                                relationship
Nothing was broken, and we made surprisingly little
                                noise.

DAVID HOLBROOK

Mending the Fire

A soft cold spring rain: where the gutter drips
I pause, waiting my time between the drops.
Over the shed roof with its grey stone-crops
A pale face at the pane, a gesture at its lips,

I wave, then you are gone, and I am in the dark,
And pause among the coal. A withered stalk
Breaks as I shovel at the wall: a paper keck
The white and viable once rooted in a crack

And grew indoors, and died, last summer, in the heat.
'Is there no more in life than this?' I think as I put out
                                        the light,
Bearing our crumb of comfort for the cool March night.
'If I am more than this dried thistle, what then, what?'

You are no longer at the window: a sudden gust
Plucks at me as I catch the latch in haste:
Then, as I walk along the house, carrying coals in, just,
I hear your voice, and the sad vacant mood is past.

But in that moment between outhouse and door
I saw our lintel break, the house drift out from shore
And sail away into a waste of time – as on the fire
We pile old forests now, or as the thistle failed to flower.

Nothing was left, as the rain rinsed my cheeks
Like unquenched tears, as by a grave grief breaks.
The new fire mends, and solemnly each makes
A love to each by glances, deeper than love that speaks.

On the Brink of a Pit

We had heard so much about Melanie already:
Couldn't eat our kind of food, our Saturday her
                                    Sabbath
Went on Friday to say her prayers, was learning
                                    Hebrew.

I took our child to her party, carrying a book-token
Covered in child-gay seals, because they love one
                                    another
And Melanie is saving to buy her great Jewish Bible.

The Sunday afternoon was full of the first bird-chimes
                                    of spring
Warm sun honeyed the suburban gardens, and
                            handsome women
Tapped over a few skeleton leaves on the muddy
                                    pavements.

Dimpled, graceful, dark-haired, a puppyish twelve,
Melanie assured me with guileless big blue eyes
Her father would bring Kate home, fondly drew her
                                    into the house.

I was suddenly overwhelmed: yet uninvolved,
A fountain of tears rose in me, misting the afternoon:
I wanted a thousand lives to worship what Melanie
                                    was –
No more than a pretty child. But all the previous night
I had wrestled with black perceptions: we are dead for
                                    ever:
We do not mourn the time before we came: being is all
                                    that matters:
Melanie's eyes my daughter loves were everything
                                    possible.

So I stood weeping unashamedly in the street in
                              Letchworth,
There being as much hate in garden cities as at
                              Majdenek,
Remembering a blurred photograph in a Polish book –

A handsome mother, like the ones who stare at me,
Clutching a child to her breast, like Melanie,
On the brink of a pit, and a storm-trooper aiming.

MOLLY HOLDEN

Stopping Places

The long car journeys to the sea
must have their breaks, not always
in towns where there's no room
to park but at the pavement's edge,
in villages, or by the woods, or in lay-bys
vibrating to the passage of fast cars.
The seat's pushed forward, the boot's lifted,
the greaseproof paper
rustles encouragingly. The children
climb to the ground and posture about,
talk, clamber on gates, eat noisily.
They're herded back, the journey
continues.
      What do you think
they'll remember most of that holiday?
the beach? the stately home?
the hot kerb of the promenade?
No. It will often be those nameless places
where they stopped, perhaps for no more
than minutes. The rank grass
and the dingy robin by the overflowing
bin for waste, the gravel ridged by
numerous wheels and the briared wood
that no one else had bothered
to explore, the long inviting field
down which there wasn't time
to go – these will stick in their memories
when beauty spots evaporate.
Was it worth the expense?
                but
these are the rewards of travelling.
There must be an end in sight
for the transient stopping places
to be necessary, to be memorable.

TED HUGHES

Witches

Once was every woman the witch
To ride a weed the ragwort road;
Devil to do whatever she would:
Each rosebud, every old bitch.

Did they bargain their bodies or no?
Proprietary the devil that
Went horsing on their every thought
When they scowled the strong and lucky low.

Dancing in Ireland nightly, gone
To Norway (the ploughboy bridled),
Nightlong under the blackamoor spraddled,
Back beside their spouse by dawn

As if they had dreamed all. Did they dream it?
Oh, our science says they did.
It was all wishfully dreamed in bed.
Small psychology would unseam it.

Bitches still sulk, rosebuds blow,
And we are devilled. And though these weep
Over our harms, who's to know
Where their feet dance while their heads sleep?

Thrushes

Terrifying are the attent sleek thrushes on the lawn,
More coiled steel than living – a poised
Dark deadly eye, those delicate legs
Triggered to stirrings beyond sense – with a start, a
                                bounce, a stab
Overtake the instant and drag out some writhing thing.
No indolent procrastinations and no yawning stares.

No sighs or head-scratchings. Nothing but bounce and
                                                    stab
And a ravening second.

Is it their single-minded-sized skulls, or a trained
Body, or genius, or a nestful of brats
Gives their days this bullet and automatic
Purpose? Mozart's brain had it, and the shark's mouth
That hungers down the blood-smell even to a leak of
                                                its own
Side and devouring of itself: efficiency which
Strikes too streamlined for any doubt to pluck at it
Or obstruction deflect.

With a man it is otherwise. Heroisms on horseback,
Outstripping his desk-diary at a broad desk,
Carving at a tiny ivory ornament
For years: his act worships itself – while for him,
Though he bends to be blent in the prayer, how loud
                                        and above what
Furious spaces of fire do the distracting devils
Orgy and hosannah, under what wilderness
Of black silent waters weep.

How Water Began to Play

Water wanted to live
It went to the sun it came weeping back
Water wanted to live
It went to the trees they burned it came weeping back
They rotted it came weeping back
Water wanted to live
It went to the flowers they crumpled it came weeping
                                                    back

It wanted to live
It went to the womb it met blood
It came weeping back
It went to the womb it met knife

106

It came weeping back
It went to the womb it met maggot and rottenness
It came weeping back it wanted to die

It went to time it went through the stone door
It came weeping back
It went searching through all space for nothingness
It came weeping back it wanted to die

Till it had no weeping left

It lay at the bottom of all things

utterly worn out   utterly clear

Roe-Deer

In the dawn-dirty light, in the biggest snow of the year
Two blue-dark deer stood in the road, alerted.

They had happened into my dimension
The moment I was arriving just there.

They planted their two or three years of secret deerhood
Clear on my snow-screen vision of the abnormal

And hesitated in the all-way disintegration
And stared at me. And so for some lasting seconds

I could think the deer were waiting for me
To remember the password and sign

That the curtain had blown aside for a moment
And there where the trees were no longer trees, nor the
                                    road a road

The deer had come for me.

Then they ducked through the hedge, and upright they
                              rode their legs
Away downhill over a snow-lonely field

Towards tree dark – finally
Seeming to eddy and glide and fly away up

Into the boil of big flakes.
The snow took them and soon their nearby hoofprints
                                    as well

Revising its dawn inspiration
Back to the ordinary.

ELIZABETH JENNINGS

Song at the Beginning of Autumn

Now watch this autumn that arrives
In smells. All looks like summer still;
Colours are quite unchanged, the air
On green and white serenely thrives.
Heavy the trees with growth and full
The fields. Flowers flourish everywhere.

Proust who collected time within
A child's cake would understand
The ambiguity of this –
Summer still raging while a thin
Column of smoke stirs from the land
Proving that autumn gropes for us.

But every season is a kind
Of rich nostalgia. We give names –
Autumn and summer, winter, spring –
As though to unfasten from the mind
Our moods and give them outward forms.
We want the certain, solid thing.

But I am carried back against
My will into a childhood where
Autumn is bonfires, marbles, smoke;
I lean against my window fenced
From evocations in the air.
When I said autumn, autumn broke.

In the Night

Out of my window late at night I gape
And see the stars but do not watch them really,
And hear the trains but do not listen clearly;
Inside my mind I turn about to keep

Myself awake, yet am not there entirely.
Something of me is out in the dark landscape.

How much am I then what I think, how much what I
feel?
How much the eye that seems to keep stars straight?
Do I control what I can contemplate
Or is it my vision that's amenable?
I turn in my mind, my mind is a room whose wall
I can see the top of but never completely scale.

All that I love is, like the night, outside,
Good to be gazed at, looking as if it could
With a simple gesture be brought inside my head
Or in my heart. But my thoughts about it divide
Me from my object. Now deep in my bed
I turn and the world turns on the other side.

Euthanasia

The law's been passed and I am lying low
Hoping to hide from those who think they are
Kindly, compassionate. My step is slow.
I hurry. Will the executioner
Be watching how I go?

Others about me clearly feel the same.
The deafest one pretends that she can hear.
The blindest hides her white stick while the lame
Attempt to stride. Life has become so dear.
Last time the doctor came,

All who could speak said they felt very well.
Did we imagine he was watching with
A new deep scrutiny? We could not tell.
Each minute now we think the stranger Death
Will take us from each cell

110

For that is what our little rooms now seem
To be. We are prepared to bear much pain,
Terror attacks us wakeful, every dream
Is now a nightmare. Doctor's due again.
We hold on to the gleam

Of sight, a word to hear. We act, we act,
And doing so we wear our weak selves out.
We said 'We want to die' once when we lacked
The chance of it. We wait in fear and doubt.
O life, you are so packed

With possibility. Old age seems good.
The ache, the anguish – we could bear them we
Declare. The ones who pray plead with their God
To turn the murdering ministers away,
But they come softly shod.

T. H. JONES

A Storm in Childhood

We had taken the long way home, a mile
Or two further than any of us had to walk,
But it meant being together longer, and home later.

The storm broke on us – broke is a cliché,
But us isn't – that storm was loosed for us, on us.
My cousin Blodwen, oldest and wisest of us,
Said in a voice we'd never heard her use before:
'The lightning kills you when it strikes the trees.'
If we were in anything besides a storm, it was trees.
On our left, the valley bottom was nothing but trees,
And on our right the trees went halfway up
The hill. We ran, between the trees and the trees,
Five children hand-in-hand, afraid of God,
Afraid of being among the lightning-fetching
Trees, soaked, soaked with rain, with sweat, with tears,
Frightened, if that's the adequate word, frightened
By the loud voice and the lambent threat,
Frightened certainly of whippings for being late,
Five children, ages six to eleven, stumbling
After a bit of running through trees from God.
Even my cousin who was eleven – I can't remember
If she was crying, too – I suppose I hope so.
But I do remember the younger ones when the
                                        stumbling
Got worse as the older terror of trees got worse
Adding their tears' irritation to the loud world of wet
And tall trees waiting to be struck by the flash, and us
With them – that running stumble, hand-in-hand – five
Children aware of our sins as we ran stumblingly:
Our sins which seemed such pointless things to talk
About to mild Miss Davies on the hard Sunday benches.

112

The lightning struck no trees, nor any of us.
I think we all got beaten; some of us got colds.
It was the longest race I ever ran,
A race against God's voice sounding from the hills
And his blaze aimed at the trees and at us,
A race in the unfriendly rain, with only the other
Children, hand-in-hand, to comfort me to know
They too were frightened, all of us miserable sinners.

JAMES KIRKUP

No More Hiroshimas

At the station exit, my bundle in hand,
Early the winter afternoon's wet snow
Falls thinly round me, out of a crudded sun.
I had forgotten to remember where I was.
Looking about, I see it might be anywhere –
A station, a town like any other in Japan,
Ramshackle, muddy, noisy, drab; a cheerfully
Shallow permanence: peeling concrete, litter, 'Atomic
Lotion, for hair fall-out', a flimsy department-store;
Racks and towers of neon, flashy over tiled and tilted
                                                waves
Of little roofs, shacks cascading lemons and
                                 persimmons,
Oranges and dark-red apples, shanties awash with
                                          rainbows
Of squid and octopus, shellfish, slabs of tuna, oysters,
                                              ice,
Ablaze with fans of soiled nude-picture books
Thumbed abstractedly by schoolboys, with second-
                                 hand looks.

The river remains unchanged, sad, refusing
                                 rehabilitation.
In this long, wide, empty official boulevard
The new trees are still small, the office blocks
Basely functional, the bridge a slick abstraction.
But the river remains unchanged, sad, refusing
                                 rehabilitation.

In the city centre, far from the station's lively squalor,
A kind of life goes on, in cinemas and hi-fi coffee bars,
In the shuffling racket of pin-table palaces and parlours,
The souvenir-shops piled with junk, kimonoed kewpie-
                                          dolls,

114

Models of the bombed Industry Promotion Hall,
                              memorial ruin
Tricked out with glitter-frost and artificial pearls.

Set in an awful emptiness, the modern tourist hotel is
                              trimmed
With jaded Christmas frippery, flatulent balloons; in the
                              hall,
A giant dingy iced cake in the shape of a Cinderella
                              coach.
The contemporary stairs are treacherous, the corridors
Deserted, my room an overheated morgue, the bar in
                              darkness.
Punctually, the electric chimes ring out across the tidy
                              waste
Their doleful public hymn – the tune unrecognizable,
                              evangelist.

Here atomic peace is geared to meet the tourist trade.
Let it remain like this, for all the world to see,
Without nobility or loveliness, and dogged with shame
That is beyond all hope of indignation. Anger, too, is
                              dead.
And why should memorials of what was far
From pleasant have the grace that helps us to forget?

In the dying afternoon, I wander dying round the Park
                              of Peace.
It is right, this squat, dead place, with its left-over air
Of an abandoned International Trade and Tourist Fair.
The stunted trees are wrapped in straw against the cold.
The gardeners are old, old women in blue bloomers,
                              white aprons,
Survivors weeding the dead brown lawns around the
                              Children's Monument.

A hideous pile, the Atomic Bomb Explosion Centre,
                              freezing cold,
'Includes the Peace Tower, a museum containing

115

Atomic-melted slates and bricks, photos showing
What the Atomic Desert looked like, and other
Relics of the catastrophe.'

The other relics:
The ones that made me weep;
The bits of burnt clothing,
The stopped watches, the torn shirts.
The twisted buttons,
The stained and tattered vests and drawers,
The ripped kimonos and charred boots,
The white blouse polka-dotted with atomic rain,
                                        indelible,
The cotton summer pants the blasted boys crawled
                              home in, to bleed
And slowly die.

Remember only these.
They are the memorials we need.
(1963)

Waiting for the Train to Start

The mysterious movement of a dream
came back to my awakened sense
that evening, in the apparent gliding
of the stationary train, in which alone
I waited, watching the slow start,
the wheel withdrawal and increasing
miracle of effort of the long, sustained
acceleration as the sleeping cars,
the dim, flickering procession
of the train that had been still
beside me, eased itself without a sign
away, in yet another stern departure.

As I watched it, from my half-dark corner,
with the other train's departure I

too seemed to move, and swiftly slide,
but in departure more than ordinary,
sadder, more intense than any past farewell.
For I, too, but in the opposite direction
was departing, with the same ingrowing
pain of speed, yet with a dream's haunted sense
of motion without feeling, speed
without the sound and energy of wings labouring
in the materials of space and time, an ever backwards
                                        hauled
propulsion, memory of birth and future things.

Soon, in this earth-borne flight,
this effortless commotion, powerless,
but faint with force that seemed to spell
a vast and irresistible vanishment,
my eyes half closed, in heavenly suspense
my weightless body came adrift,
and on a wind's great soundless sea
of sense and spirit it was smoothly launched . . .
Until time and the final carriage crashed
reality awake again. As if from a real dream
from real heights out of myself I leaped, and fell
back into stationary blackness, and my heart's loud hell.

PHILIP LARKIN

Church Going

Once I am sure there's nothing going on
I step inside, letting the door thud shut.
Another church: matting, seats, and stone,
And little books; sprawlings of flowers, cut
For Sunday, brownish now; some brass and stuff
Up at the holy end; the small neat organ;
And a tense, musty, unignorable silence,
Brewed God knows how long. Hatless, I take off
My cycle-clips in awkward reverence,

Move forward, run my hand around the font.
From where I stand, the roof looks almost new –
Cleaned, or restored? Someone would know: I don't.
Mounting the lectern, I peruse a few
Hectoring large-scale verses, and pronounce
'Here endeth' much more loudly than I'd meant.
The echoes snigger briefly. Back at the door
I sign the book, donate an Irish sixpence,
Reflect the place was not worth stopping for.

Yet stop I did: in fact I often do,
And always end much at a loss like this,
Wondering what to look for; wondering, too,
When churches fall completely out of use
What we shall turn them into, if we shall keep
A few cathedrals chronically on show,
Their parchment, plate and pyx in locked cases,
And let the rest rent-free to rain and sheep.
Shall we avoid them as unlucky places?

Or, after dark, will dubious women come
To make their children touch a particular stone;
Pick simples for a cancer; or on some
Advised night see walking a dead one?

118

Power of some sort or other will go on
In games, in riddles, seemingly at random;
But superstition, like belief, must die,
And what remains when disbelief has gone?
Grass, weedy pavement, brambles, buttress, sky,

A shape less recognizable each week,
A purpose more obscure. I wonder who
Will be the last, the very last, to seek
This place for what it was; one of the crew
That tap and jot and know what rood-lofts were?
Some ruin-bibber, randy for antique,
Or Christmas-addict, counting on a whiff
Of gown-and-bands and organ-pipes and myrrh?
Or will he be my representative,

Bored, uninformed, knowing the ghostly silt
Dispersed, yet tending to this cross of ground
Through suburb scrub because it held unspilt
So long and equably what since is found
Only in separation – marriage, and birth,
And death, and thoughts of these – for whom was built
This special shell? For, though I've no idea
What this accoutred frowsty barn is worth,
It pleases me to stand in silence here;

A serious house on serious earth it is,
In whose blent air all our compulsions meet,
Are recognized, and robed as destinies.
And that much never can be obsolete,
Since someone will forever be surprising
A hunger in himself to be more serious,
And gravitating with it to this ground,
Which, he once heard, was proper to grow wise in,
If only that so many dead lie round.

At Grass

The eye can hardly pick them out
From the cold shade they shelter in,
Till wind distresses tail and mane;
Then one crops grass, and moves about
– The other seeming to look on –
And stands anonymous again.

Yet fifteen years ago, perhaps
Two dozen distances sufficed
To fable them: faint afternoons
Of Cups and Stakes and Handicaps,
Whereby their names were artificed
To inlay faded, classic Junes –

Silks at the start: against the sky
Numbers and parasols: outside,
Squadrons of empty cars, and heat,
And littered grass: then the long cry
Hanging unhushed till it subside
To stop-press columns on the street.

Do memories plague their ears like flies?
They shake their heads. Dusk brims the shadows.
Summer by summer all stole away,
The starting-gates, the crowds and cries –
All but the unmolesting meadows.
Almanacked, their names live; they

Have slipped their names, and stand at ease,
Or gallop for what must be joy,
And not a fieldglass sees them home,
Or curious stop-watch prophesies:
Only the groom, and the groom's boy,
With bridles in the evening come.

Sad Steps

Groping back to bed after a piss
I part thick curtains, and am startled by
The rapid clouds, the moon's cleanliness.

Four o'clock: wedge-shadowed gardens lie
Under a cavernous, a wind-picked sky.
There's something laughable about this,

The way the moon dashes through clouds that blow
Loosely as cannon-smoke to stand apart
(Stone-coloured light sharpening the roofs below)

High and preposterous and separate –
Lozenge of love! Medallion of art!
O wolves of memory! Immensements! No,

One shivers slightly, looking up there.
The hardness and the brightness and the plain
Far-reaching singleness of that wide stare

Is a reminder of the strength and pain
Of being young; that it can't come again,
But is for others undiminished somewhere.

The Whitsun Weddings

That Whitsun, I was late getting away:
    Not till about
One-twenty on the sunlit Saturday
Did my three-quarters-empty train pull out,
All windows down, all cushions hot, all sense
Of being in a hurry gone. We ran
Behind the backs of houses, crossed a street
Of blinding windscreens, smelt the fish-dock; thence
The river's level drifting breadth began,
Where sky and Lincolnshire and water meet.

121

All afternoon, through the tall heat that slept
  For miles inland,
A slow and stopping curve southwards we kept.
Wide farms went by, short-shadowed cattle, and
Canals with floatings of industrial froth;
A hothouse flashed uniquely: hedges dipped
And rose: and now and then a smell of grass
Displaced the reek of buttoned carriage-cloth
Until the next town, new and nondescript,
Approached with acres of dismantled cars.

At first, I didn't notice what a noise
  The weddings made
Each station that we stopped at: sun destroys
The interest of what's happening in the shade,
And down the long cool platforms whoops and skirls
I took for porters larking with the mails,
And went on reading. Once we started, though,
We passed them, grinning and pomaded, girls
In parodies of fashion, heels and veils,
All posed irresolutely, watching us go,

As if out on the end of an event
  Waving good-bye
To something that survived it. Struck, I leant
More promptly out next time, more curiously,
And saw it all again in different terms:
The fathers with broad belts under their suits
And seamy foreheads; mothers loud and fat;
An uncle shouting smut; and then the perms,
The nylon gloves and jewellery-substitutes,
The lemons, mauves, and olive-ochres that

Marked off the girls unreally from the rest.
  Yes, from cafés
And banquet-halls up yards, and bunting-dressed
Coach-party annexes, the wedding-days
Were coming to an end. All down the line
Fresh couples climbed aboard: the rest stood round;

122

The last confetti and advice were thrown,
And, as we moved, each face seemed to define
Just what it saw departing: children frowned
At something dull; fathers had never known

Success so huge and wholly farcical;
    The women shared
The secret like a happy funeral;
While girls, gripping their handbags tighter, stared
At a religious wounding. Free at last,
And loaded with the sum of all they saw,
We hurried towards London, shuffling gouts of steam.
Now fields were building-plots, and poplars cast
Long shadows over major roads, and for
Some fifty minutes, that in time would seem

Just long enough to settle hats and say
    I nearly died,
A dozen marriages got under way.
They watched the landscape, sitting side by side
An Odeon went past, a cooling tower,
And someone running up to bowl – and none
Thought of the others they would never meet
Or how their lives would all contain this hour.
I thought of London spread out in the sun,
Its postal districts packed like squares of wheat:

There we were aimed. And as we raced across
    Bright knots of rail
Past standing Pullmans, walls of blackened moss
Came close, and it was nearly done, this frail
Travelling coincidence; and what it held
Stood ready to be loosed with all the power
That being changed can give. We slowed again,
And as the tightened brakes took hold, there swelled
A sense of falling, like an arrow-shower
Sent out of sight, somewhere becoming rain.

Bridal

You've felt this before – eyes wide open
  In a strange bedroom, pitch-black,
A moment's panic till the soul slides back
  Into the body, or again
Mid-sentence as you gather in the slack
Of a circuitous argument, to crush
  An enemy, when suddenly you find
That brilliant *coup de grâce* has slipped your mind,
  Leaving you stranded, a cruel hush
Descending, as you feel the seconds grind

Down to a halt . . . So it is you stand
  Jarred out of memory, beside
This veiled apotheosis of a bride,
  Your hand held up beside her hand,
Lily-of-the-Valley bunched above the wide
Cream wake of tulle that ripples through a sea
  Of faces so similar they clash
Like adjacent notes – faces in lavish
  Frames of burnished fur and millinery,
Metallic faces, vulcanised in cash –

Money, breeding, the lace-covered prize
  Rustling like a big white rose;
Prime of England – and what if, blind, you chose
  What others crave with open eyes –
Stoles, medals, diamonds – how can you refuse?
Golden, laburnum-fringed, the organ pipes
  Drown hesitation in a great swell
Of sound that sends a tremor through her veil;
  How can you wait to taste those lips,
Taste acquiescence on your tongue? 'I will,

I do' – words in a confetti swirl
    Dissolve the present, and thrust
You forward into daylight while the dust
    Of a life left starts to settle:
You stand and blink, a man without a past –
Choice was illusion too; look how the father
    Looms up from a dazzling winter sun –
Grin of a species welcoming its own;
    One hand on your shoulder, in the other
A champagne bottle smoking like a gun.

LIZ LOCHHEAD

Revelation

I remember once being shown the black bull
when a child at the farm for eggs and milk.
They called him Bob – as though perhaps
you could reduce a monster
with the charm of a friendly name.
At the threshold of his outhouse, someone
held my hand and let me peer inside.
At first, only black
and the hot reek of him. Then he was immense,
his edges merging with the darkness, just
a big bulk and a roar to be really scared of,
a trampling, and a clanking tense with the chain's jerk.
His eyes swivelled in the great wedge of his tossed
                                        head.
He roared his rage. His nostrils gaped.

And in the yard outside,
oblivious hens picked their way about.
The faint and rather festive tinkling
behind the mellow stone and hasp was all they knew
of that Black Mass, straining at his chains.
I had always half-known he existed –
this antidote and Anti-Christ his anarchy
threatening the eggs, well rounded, self-contained –
and the placidity of milk.

I ran, my pigtails thumping on my back in fear,
past the big boys in the farm lane
who pulled the wings from butterflies and
blew up frogs with straws.
Past throned hedge and harried nest,
scared of the eggs shattering –
only my small and shaking hand on the jug's rim
in case the milk should spill.

126

Song of Solomon

You
smell nice he said
what is it?
Honey? He nuzzled a soap-trace
in the hollow of her collarbone.
The herbs of her hair?
Salt? He licked
a riverbed between her breasts.

(He'd seemed
not unconvinced by the chemical
attar of roses at her armpit. She tried
to relax have absolute faith in
the expensive secretions of teased civet to
trust the musk at her pulse spots
never think of the whiff of
sourmilk from her navel
the curds of cheese between the toes
the dried blood smell of many small wounds
the stink of fish at her crotch.)

No there he was above her apparently
as happy as a hog rooting for truffles.
She caressed him behind the ear
with the garlic of her cooking-thumb.
She banged shut her eyes
and hoped he would not smell her fear.

MICHAEL LONGLEY

Wounds

Here are two pictures from my father's head —
I have kept them like secrets until now:
First, the Ulster Division at the Somme
Going over the top with 'Fuck the Pope!'
'No Surrender!': a boy about to die,
Screaming 'Give 'em one for the Shankill!'
'Wilder than Gurkhas' were my father's words
Of admiration and bewilderment.
Next comes the London-Scottish padre
Resettling kilts with his swagger-stick,
With a stylish backhand and a prayer.
Over a landscape of dead buttocks
My father followed him for fifty years.
At last, a belated casualty,
He said — lead traces flaring till they hurt —
'I am dying for King and Country, slowly.'
I touched his hand, his thin head I touched.

Now, with military honours of a kind,
With his badges, his medals like rainbows,
His spinning compass, I bury beside him
Three teenage soldiers, bellies full of
Bullets and Irish beer, their flies undone.
A packet of Woodbines I throw in,
A lucifer, the Sacred Heart of Jesus
Paralysed as heavy guns put out
The night-light in a nursery for ever;
Also a bus-conductor's uniform —
He collapsed beside his carpet-slippers
Without a murmur, shot through the head
By a shivering boy who wandered in
Before they could turn the television down
Or tidy away the supper dishes.
To the children, to a bewildered wife,
I think 'Sorry Missus' was what he said.

GEORGE MACBETH

Poem for Breathing

Trudging through drifts along the hedge, we
Probe at the flecked, white essence with sticks. Across
    The hill field, mushroom-brown in
    The sun, the mass of the sheep trundle
As though on small wheels. With a jerk, the farmer

    Speaks, quietly pleased. *Here's one.* And we
Hunch round while he digs. Dry snow flies like castor
    Sugar from the jabbing edge
    Of the spade. The head rubs clear first, a
Yellow cone with eyes. The farmer leans, panting,

    On the haft. *Will you grab him from the*
Front? I reach down, grope for greasy fur, rough, neat
    Ears. I grip at shoulders, while
    He heaves at the coarse, hairy
Backside. With a clumsy lug, it's up, scrambling
    For a hold on the white, soft grass. It
Stares round, astonished to be alive. Then it
    Runs, like a rug on legs, to
    Join the shy others. Ten dark little
Pellets of dung steam in the hole, where it lay

    Dumped, and sank in. *You have to probe with*
The pole along the line of the rest of the
    Hedge. They tend to be close. We
    Probe, floundering in Wellingtons, breath
Rasping hard in the cold. The released one is

    All right. He has found his pen in the
Sun. I dig in the spade's thin haft, close to barbed
    Wire. Someone else speaks. *Here's*
    Another. And it starts again. The
Rush to see, the leaning sense of hush, and the

Snow-flutter as we grasp for the quick
Life buried in the ivory ground. *There were*
    Ninety eight, and I counted
    Ninety five. That means one more. And I
Kneel to my spade, feeling the chill seep through my

    Boots. The sun burns dark. I imagine
The cold-worn ears, the legs bunched in the foetus
    Position for warmth. I smell
    The feathery, stale white duvet, the
Hot air from the nostrils, burning upwards. And

    I crouch above the sheep, hunched in its
Briar bunk below the hedge. From the field, it
    Hears the bleat of its friends, their
    Far joy. It feels only the cushions
Of frost on its frozen back. I breathe, slowly,

    Trying to melt that hard-packed snow. I
Breathe, melting a little snow with my breath. If
    Everyone in the whole
    World would breathe here, it might help. Breathe
Here a little, as you read, it might still help.

In Love with Red

    For years, I liked it least.
        It seemed so bold,
Strident and brassy, tinny at the worst,
A colour for the crude, the flashy ones,
        A slavering beast
  Of the palette, raging flame with gold,
        Something to burst
The eardrums, and explode like firework suns.

    Now I know better. Home
        After three days
Of living in the meekness of dull stone

130

That London is, I turn to praise pure red.
      Seeing you comb
  A line of carmine to a glaze
      I want to atone
To all scarlet richness for my former dread.

      I've come of age. This heat
       Of hue, that flares
In uniforms and holocausts, needs time.
Such blood of poppies by the late June roads!
      Now as I meet
  Red everywhere, with flagrant stares,
      Watching it climb,
I grant its depth, pulse leaping like a toad's.

      At our party, I'll wear red,
      Mess-red with gold,
And flaunt amongst the rest, red's paladins.
I'll be an acolyte of vivid hue,
      And let the dead
  Lie dim and simple in their cold.
      A time for grins
Is come, for jousting crimson, all things new.

A Field of Rape

Each year I see one, yellow in the distance,
About the same week, early or mid-April,
A coat of gold, a cloth of burning flame.

No-one has thrown it there, or fashioned it
As mantling for a queen, or heraldry,
Or even as the carpet for a fair.

It seres, like mustard. Like a painter's panel
Arranged in abstract to adorn the green,
Or sombre ochre, of our fenland spring.

131

I watch it from the train, or from a car,
Idling in neutral, or at fifty-five,
Or hurtling at high speed for Lynn, or London.

A field of rape, I say. I know it is
Only a cattle's crop of brassica
To feed the quiet ruminants in winter.

Yes, but it burns. It takes the eye in fire
And rages on the rolling down, or flat
For acre upon acre, dazzling hue.

I touch it in my dreams. I bend, and wade
Through hock-high meadows of its rustling silk
With scents of byre and honey in my nostrils.

Reaching, I chew. Retching, I vomit up
All the unconscious essence of desire
And hawk, and weep, amidst the tottering calves.

I fall upon my face, on cattle pats.
Deep in my dream the rape is close and hot
And what was beautiful at yellow distance

Here in the stalky stubble, thick with dung,
Amazes now no more than sainfoin cake,
Or troughs of wurzels, or the cast lucerne.

ALASDAIR MACLEAN

Rams

Their horns are pure baroque,
as thick at the root as a man's wrist.
They have golden eyes and roman noses.
All the ewes love them.

They are well equipped to love back.
In their prime they balance;
the sex at one end of their bodies
equalling the right to use it at the other.

When two of them come face to face
in the mating season
a spark jumps the gap.
Their heads drive forward like cannon balls.
Solid granite hills splinter into echoes.

They never wrestle, as stags and bulls do.
They slug it out. The hardest puncher wins.
Sometimes they back up so far for a blow
they lose sight of one another
and just start grazing.

They are infinitely and indefatigably stupid.
You can rescue the same one
from the same bramble bush
fifty times.
Such a massive casing to guard such a tiny brain –
as if Fort Knox were built to house a single penny!

But year by year those horns add growth.
The sex is outstripped in the end;
the balance tilts in the direction of the head.
I found a ram dead once.
It was trapped by the forefeet

in the dark water of a peatbog,
drowned before help could arrive
by the sheer weight of its skull.
Maiden ewes were grazing near it,
immune to its clangorous lust.
It knelt on the bank, hunched over its own image,
its great head buried in the great head facing it.
Its horns, going forward in the old way,
had battered through at last to the other side.

In Time of 'The Breaking of Nations'

It's in the corners of the galleries one finds them,
where it's dark,
those old Dutch genre paintings,
hung there in Victorian days
after so many vapourings and faintings,
after such loosening of stays.
For in them nearly always,
as one's guarantee,
some peasant has held up his game of bowls
and quite without remark
walked off to pee.

Not far, of course.
It isn't delicacy he has in view.
The nearest bit of shady wall will do
where he may lean and cool his forehead
while he waits for confirmation to come through.
Indeed, for the better savouring of this hour
he has topped up his bladder well beyond its measure.
His muscles seal the opening an exquisite moment more
then 'Ah!' he goes 'Ah!' in sheer pleasure.
Good luck to him!
I think that in a world
where bigger heads come daily in on platters
he is his own continuation,
having grasped what matters.

134

It pleases me to see him there
while in the same painting
but under a different sky
Napoleon or whatever his name was then
thunders helplessly by.

Question and Answer

'Do you love me? Do you love me?'
Your voice goes on and on
like a trailhound giving tongue.
'Say you love me then. I want to hear you say it.'
I say that once, when I was very young,
I saw a rat caught in a trap,
in a wire cage, squealing and snapping.
The cage was lowered into a tank of water.
I watched the stream of bubbles ease off
and at long last stop
and when the cage was hoisted to the top
the dead rat dangled from the roof,
its jaws so firmly clenched around the wire
they had to be levered free.

But I say all this to myself;
to you I mutter, sullenly but truthfully,
the words you want to hear.
Made easy then, you turn your back for sleep
and I lie where my love has left me,
a half-formed sadness in my bones
that will not waste or keep
and all around the water filling,
rising year by year,
and getting darker still above me,
getting dark and very deep.

Cloud shout

It was a tremendous shout,
volleying down from the clouds or thereabouts,
wordless, mostly, you would have said,
just pure frustrated energy,
a great roar of anger
such as you might loose off
at the sheer intractability of things, or at someone
who was stupidly making a fool of you.

Spreading hay at the far end of the meadow
I cowered and covered. My clothes lifted, drummed.
A solid push of sound
went crashing through the uncut grass,
breaking on the drystone wall, picking up again
and splintering finally into echoes
far up the hillside.

On the adjoining farm I saw my neighbour's wife,
at the epicentre, so it seemed, blown naked,
spinning and whining like a top, a white top,
drilling into the ground, her lit hair circling her.

Afterwards, silence.
I stood stupidly in the blasted field,
my blood careering through my heart,
hearing the prongs of the hayfork sing in my hands,
hearing all around me
the small thudding-down of featherless, cooked birds.

DEREK MAHON

The Return
(*for John Hewitt*)

I am saying goodbye to the trees,
The beech, the cedar, the elm,
The mild woods of these parts
Misted with car exhaust,
And sawdust, and the last
Gasps of the poisoned nymphs.

I have watched girls walking
And children playing under
Lilac and rhododendron,
And me flicking my ash
Into the rose bushes
As if I owned the place;

As if the trees responded
To my ignorant admiration
Before dawn when the branches
Glitter at first light,
Or later on when the finches
Disappear for the night;

And often thought if I lived
Long enough in this house
I would turn into a tree
Like somebody in Ovid
– A small tree certainly
But a tree nonetheless –

Perhaps befriend the oak,
The chestnut and the yew,
Become a home for birds,
A shelter for the nymphs,
And gaze out over the downs
As if I belonged here too.

But where I am going the trees
Are few and far between.
No richly forested slopes,
Not for a long time,
And few winking woodlands;
There are no nymphs to be seen.

Out there you would look in vain
For a rose bush; but find,
Rooted in stony ground,
A last stubborn growth
Battered by constant rain
And twisted by the sea-wind

With nothing to recommend it
But its harsh tenacity
Between the blinding windows
And the forests of the sea,
As if its very existence
Were a reason to continue.

Crone, crow, scarecrow,
Its worn fingers scrabbling
At a torn sky, it stands
On the edge of everything
Like a burnt-out angel
Raising petitionary hands.

Grotesque by day, at twilight
An almost tragic figure
Of anguish and despair,
It merges into the funeral
Cloud-continent of night
As if it belongs there.

Lingfield-Coleraine, 1977

138

The Snow Party
(*for Louis Asekoff*)

Bashō, coming
To the city of Nagoya,
Is asked to a snow party.

There is a tinkling of china
And tea into china;
There are introductions.

Then everyone
Crowds to the window
To watch the falling snow.

Snow is falling on Nagoya
And farther south
On the tiles of Kyōto.

Eastward, beyond Irago,
It is falling
Like leaves on the cold sea.

Elsewhere they are burning
Witches and heretics
In the boiling squares,

Thousands have died since dawn
In the service
Of barbarous kings;

But there is silence
In the houses of Nagoya
And the hills of Ise.

Achill

im chaonaí uaigneach nach mór go bhfeicim an lá

I lie and imagine a first light gleam in the bay
   After one more night of erosion and nearer the grave,
Then stand and gaze from a window at break of day
   As a shearwater skims the ridge of an incoming wave;
And I think of my son a dolphin in the Aegean,
   A sprite among sails knife-bright in a seasonal wind,
And wish he were here where currachs walk on the
                                        ocean
   To ease with his talk the solitude locked in my mind.

I sit on a stone after lunch and consider the glow
   Of the sun through mist, a pearl bulb containèdly
                                     fierce;
A rain-shower darkens the schist for a minute or so
   Then it drifts away and the sloe-black patches disperse.
Croagh Patrick towers like Naxos over the water
   And I think of my daughter at work on her difficult
                                     art
And wish she were with me now between thrush and
                                    plover,
   Wild thyme and sea-thrift, to lift the weight from my
                                    heart.

The young sit smoking and laughing on the bridge at
                                    evening
   Like birds on a telephone pole or notes on a score.
A tin whistle squeals in the parlour, once more it is
                                    raining,
   Turfsmoke inclines and a wind whines under the door;
And I lie and imagine the lights going on in the harbour
   Of white-housed Náousa, your clear definition at
                                    night,
And wish you were here to upstage my disconsolate
                                    labour
   As I glance through a few thin pages and switch off
                                    the light.

GERDA MAYER

Sir Brooke Boothby

(after the painting by Joseph Wright of Derby, 1781)

Sir Brooke, reclining by a brook,
How punningly your lines flow
Beside your namesake. Time has changed
The leaves to autumn overhead.
You clasp Rousseau.

And all your nature's heraldry
Is here set out. It is your look –
Voluptuous, thoughtful, quizzical, –
Has puzzled me for many years,
Belov'd Sir Brooke.

Two years ago they cleaned you up.
Still sensuous, you leer the less,
No longer the seducer but
Hinting of sorrows yet to come,
And pensiveness.

Yet still amused, – you scrutinise
Me as intently as I you.
Dumpy and old, I've fared the worse.
Will others come when I am gone,
Or be as true?

My very sparkling Brooke, we are
Two centuries and Styx apart.
Yet mirror-imaged our loss
(Your child, my father) and we share
A love for art.

It would be pleasant if we were
Among the leaves so juxtaposed

You on the left, I on the right
That you would flow above me when
The book was closed.

Lucky

All things bright and beautiful
you loved your blameless cat
his name was LUCKY
lucky cat
fluffy and fat
a friend to all
and pure in thought word and deed

One night his luck ran out
chatted up, bundled off, sold
to men in white coats

Shaved from the neck to the end of his tail
Lucky was immersed
for twentyone days on end
in cold water
How long can he last
before going numb in his mind?

The other cats thought he was lucky
they were off their food
with the shocks

The puppy dog's head
on the old dog's neck
thought Lucky was lucky

The rats thought so
weeping blood

And so did the monkey
swinging in space

142

(later awarded the
V.D., T.B., and Order of Radiation)

And so did the newts
when their eyes were cut out
the better to see whether they needed them

And the cattle
in stocks
and the hens
in irons
every hope rolling away from them
they all thought Lucky was lucky

And he was
he died
God's last mercy

Watch it Lucky
even now
somebody
licensed to kill
by degrees
is working on
Eternal Life

Make Believe

Say I were not sixty,
say you weren't near-hundred,
say you were alive.
Say my verse was read
in some distant country,
and say you were idly turning the pages:

The blood washed from your shirt,
the tears from your eyes,
the earth from your bones;

neither missing since 1940,
nor dead as reported later
by a friend of a friend of a friend . . .

Quite dapper you stand in that bookshop
and chance upon my clues.

That is why at sixty
when some publisher asks me
for biographical details,
I still carefully give
the year of my birth,
the name of my hometown:

GERDA MAYER born '27, in Karlsbad,
Czechoslovakia . . . write to me, father.

NOTE: The author's father, Arnold Stein, escaped from the
German concentration camp in Nisko in 1939, fled to Russian-
occupied Lemberg/Lwow, and then disappeared in the
summer of 1940. It is thought he may have died in a Russian
camp.

144

ROGER MCGOUGH

Prayer to Saint Grobianus

The patron saint of coarse people

Intercede for us dear saint we beseech thee
    We fuzzdutties and cullions
    Dunderwhelps and trollybags
    Lobcocks and loobies.

On our behalf seek divine forgiveness for
    We puzzlepates and pigsconces
    Ninnyhammers and humgruffins
    Gossoons and clapperdudgeons.

Have pity on we poor wretched sinners
    We blatherskites and lopdoodles
    Lickspiggots and clinchpoops
    Quibberdicks and Quakebuttocks.

Free us from the sorrows of this world
And grant eternal happiness in the next
    We snollygosters and gundyguts
    Gongoozlers and groutheads
    Ploots, quoobs, lurds and swillbellies.

As it was in the beginning, is now, and ever shall be,
World without end. OK?

MEDBH MCGUCKIAN

To the Nightingale

I remember our first night in this grey
And paunchy house: you were still slightly
In love with me, and dreamt of having
A grown son, your body in the semi-gloom
Turning my dead layers into something
Resembling a rhyme. That smart and
Cheerful rain almost beat the hearing
Out of me, and yet I heard my name
Pronounced in a whisper as a June day
Will force itself into every room.

To the nightingale it made no difference
Of course, that you tossed about an hour,
Two hours, till what was left of your future
Began: nor to the moon that nearly rotted,
Like the twenty-first century growing
Its grass through me. But became in the end,
While you were still asleep, a morning
Where I saw our neighbours' mirabelle,
Bent over our hedge, and its trespassing
Fruit, unacknowledged as our own.

ROBERT MINHINNICK

Short Wave

I try to tune in, but Europe's blurred voice
Becomes stranger with the movement of the dial.

All stations seem to give a fragment of
Performance – Mozart disarmed by a fizzled
Prodigy; innumerable cliques of wordsmiths.

As the electric crackles I make believe
I am composing an avant-garde symphony,
A sound poem for a hall of idiot speech.

But behind the static are moments of sanity:
A string quartet and interesting chanteuse,
Then histrionics at a play's climax.

For some reason, a hubbub of languages
And dim music becomes more important
Than any scheduled programme. It suits

My mood perhaps, this indecipherable mayhem
Of newscasters and sopranos, and the long
Returns to electronic gibbering.

Somewhere, behind a rockband's sudden squall,
A morse message is tapped out. For a few seconds
It is clear, articulate, before melting

Into Europe's verbiage. It was not mayday.
And I twist the dial a hairsbreadth into jazz.

Sunday Morning

I choose back lanes for the pace they will impose,
    An old perspective half forgotten
Surprising me now as the world slows
With these things the broad road lacked:
    Carboys of vitriol stacked in a garage,
Orange hooks of honeysuckle gripping a wall.

Here a church window becomes an arch of light
    And the pitching of a hymn a brief
Infusion of the air. Voices, and low
Indistinguishable words, the organ's bass
    The foundation for a ritual
I trespass in, that suddenly

Intensifies the day. On the other side
    I picture them: the ranked devout
Pulling the ribbons from the black prayerbooks
And each with his or her accustomed doubt
    Submitting to a poetry
Triumphant as the church's muscular brass.

Thus Sunday morning: a gleaning
    Of its strange wisdoms. The certainty
Of hymns comes with me through a different town
Of derelict courts and gardens, a stable
    Where a vizored man beats sparks from a wheel,
An old man splitting marble in a mason's yard,

The creamy splinters falling into my mind
    Like the heavy fragments of hymns,
Then walking on, much further, this morning being
                      Sunday.

ADRIAN MITCHELL

Fifteen Million Plastic Bags

I was walking in a government warehouse
Where the daylight never goes.
I saw fifteen million plastic bags
Hanging in a thousand rows.

Five million bags were six feet long
Five million were five foot five
Five million were stamped with Mickey Mouse
And they came in a smaller size.

Were they for guns or uniforms
Or a dirty kind of party game?
Then I saw each bag had a number
And every bag bore a name.

And five million bags were six feet long
Five million were five foot five
Five million were stamped with Mickey Mouse
And they came in a smaller size

So I've taken my bag from the hanger
And I've pulled it over my head
And I'll wait for the priest to zip it
So the radiation won't spread

Now five million bags are six feet long
Five million are five foot five
Five million are stamped with Mickey Mouse
And they come in a smaller size.

EDWIN MORGAN

Strawberries

There were never strawberries
like the ones we had
that sultry afternoon
sitting on the step
of the open french window
facing each other
your knees held in mine
the blue plates in our laps
the strawberries glistening
in the hot sunlight
we dipped them in sugar
looking at each other
not hurrying the feast
for one to come
the empty plates
laid on the stone together
with the two forks crossed
and I bent towards you
sweet in that air
in my arms
abandoned like a child
from your eager mouth
the taste of strawberries
in my memory
lean back again
let me love you

let the sun beat
on our forgetfulness
one hour of all
the heat intense
and summer lightning
on the Kilpatrick hills

let the storm wash the plates

150

The First Men on Mercury

—We come in peace from the third planet.
Would you take us to your leader?

—Bawr stretter! Bawr. Bawr. Stretterhawl?

—This is a little plastic model
of the solar system, with working parts.
You are here and we are there and we
are now here with you, is this clear?

—Gawl horrop. Bawr. Abawrhannahanna!

—Where we come from is blue and white
with brown, you see we call the brown
here 'land', the blue is 'sea', and the white
is 'clouds' over land and sea, we live
on the surface of the brown land,
all round is sea and clouds. We are 'men'.
Men come—

—Glawp men! Gawrbenner menko. Menhawl?

—Men come in peace from the third planet
which we call 'earth'. We are earthmen.
Take us earthmen to your leader.

—Thmen? Thmen? Bawr. Bawrhossop.
Yuleeda tan hanna. Harrabost yuleeda.

—I am the yuleeda. You see my hands,
we carry no benner, we come in peace.
The spaceways are all stretterhawn.

—Glawn peacemen all horrabhanna tantko!
Tan come at'mstrossop. Glawp yuleeda!

—Atoms are peacegawl in our harraban.
Menbat worrabost from tan hannahanna.

—You men we know bawrhossoptant. Bawr.
We know yuleeda. Go strawg backspetter quick.

—We cantantabawr, tantingko backspetter now!

—Banghapper now! Yes, third planet back.
Yuleeda will go back blue, white, brown
nowhanna! There is no more talk.

—Gawl han fasthapper?

—No. You must go back to your planet.
Go back in peace, take what you have gained
but quickly.

—Stretterworra gawl, gawl . . .

—Of course, but nothing is ever the same,
now is it? You'll remember Mercury.

BLAKE MORRISON

On Sizewell Beach

There are four beach huts, numbered 13 to 16,
each with net curtains and a lock.
Who owns them, what happened to the first twelve,
whether there are plans for further building:
there's no one here today to help with such enquiries,
the café closed up for the winter,
no cars or buses in the PAY AND DISPLAY.
The offshore rig is like a titan's diving board.
I've heard the rumours that it's warmer here
for bathing than at any other point along the coast.
Who started them? The same joker who bought
the village pub and named it the Vulcan,
'God of fire and metalwork and hammers,
deformed and buffoonish, a forger of rich thrones'?
Whoever he is, whatever he was up to,
he'd be doused today, like these men out back,
shooting at clay pigeons, the rain in their Adnams beer.
And now a movement on the shingle
that's more than the scissoring of terns:
a fishing boat's landed, three men in yellow waders
guiding it shorewards over metal-ribbed slats
which they lay in front of it like offerings
while the winch in its hut, tense and oily,
hauls at the hook in the prow, the smack with its catch
itself become a catch, though when I lift
the children up to see the lockjaws of sole and whiting
there's nothing in there but oilskin and rope.

I love this place, its going on with life
in the shadow of the slab behind it,
which you almost forget, or might take for a giant's
                                        Lego set,
so neat are the pipes and the chain-mail fences,
the dinky railway track running off to Leiston,

the pylons like a line of cross-country skiers,
the cooling ponds and turbine halls and reactor control
                                                      rooms
where they prove with geigers on Open Days
('Adults and Children over 14 years only')
that sealed plutonium is less radioactive than a watch.

One rain-glossed Saturday in April
a lad from Halesworth having passed his test
and wanting to impress his girlfriend
came here in the Ford he'd borrowed from his father
and took the corner much too fast, too green to judge
the danger or simply not seeing the child
left on the pavement by the father – no less reckless –
who had crossed back to his Renault for the notebook
he'd stupidly forgotten, the one with jottings
for a poem about nuclear catastrophe,
a poem later abandoned, in place of which
he'd write of the shock of turning round
to find a car had come between him and his daughter,
an eternity of bodywork blotting out the view,
a cloud or an eclipse which hangs before the eyes
and darkens all behind them, clearing at last
to the joy of finding her still standing there,
the three of us spared that other life we dream of
where the worst has already happened
and we are made to dwell forever on its shore.

ANDREW MOTION

From Bloodlines

1. Bro

We walked the way we had seen
our elders and betters walk
on their and their families' land:
with a head-back swaggering stride,
our hands stuffed deep in our pockets,

and pushed through a scraggy hedge
in the pewter afternoon light
to come to a spongy meadow
dotted with carious Cotswold boulders.
They'd told us to disappear

and discover the source of the Thames,
making us think we might find
a god stretched in a thicket
whose mouth was a massive O
spewing the river out into the grass.

But someone had stolen the god,
or maybe he never existed.
Instead we came to a patch
of stubbly reed where water
convulsed like a catch of mackerel,

and this, we supposed, was it.
We knew there was nothing to do
but quickly to match the pretence
of our head-back brazen approach
with a faked-up sense of arrival,

and stood there in silence a while,
watching the water swallow its tails.

Whatever came into your mind
was something you never said then,
and soon it was too late to ask

since a matter of days after that
I was parcelled away to school,
and took, as if it belonged to me,
the thought of the river collecting
the strength of a million ditches

hungrily under the ground,
emerging to shoulder through Lechlade,
and Oxford, and London, oily with prints
of tug-boats, and hurrying half-blind faces
peering from bridges, and giggling couples

throwing in twigs and watching them
wriggle from sight in curdling eddies,
and marvellous nineteenth-century walls
built right at the water's edge, so the eyes
of their gargoyles stare at themselves for ever.

From 'This Is Your Subject Speaking'

The last place we met
(*If I'm lucky I'll know*
which is the last;

unlucky, I mean)
was the Nursing Home:
golden afternoon light,

a hot boxed-in corridor
tiled with lime-green carpet,
the door to your room ajar

156

and you in your linen suit
watching the Test on telly.
In the silence after applause

or laconic reports, your voice
was the cold, flat voice
of someone describing someone

they hardly knew.
*Nobody's said what's wrong
and I haven't asked. Don't you.*

*Well I've nothing to live for,
have I? Christ, don't answer.
You'll tell me I have. Like seeing*

*Becker at Wimbledon, winning.
He looked just like young Auden.
That was good. I'm sure I'll die*

*when I'm as old as my father.
Which gives me until Christmas.
I simply can't cheer up –*

*and don't you start.
And don't you go, please, either,
till after my exercise . . .*

Like skaters terrified their ice
might crack, we shuffled round
the dazzling patch of lawn

and fed each other lines:
how warm it was; how fast
the daisies grew; how difficult

low branches on an apple tree
made reaching the four corners –
anything which might slow down

the easy journey
to your room, the corridor again,
and then the glass front door.

The trouble is, I've written
scenes like this so many times
there's nothing to surprise me.

But that doesn't help one bit.
It just appals me. Now you go.
I won't come out. I'll watch you.

So you did: both hands lifted
palms out, fingers spread –
more like someone shocked

or fending something off
in passive desperation
than like someone waving –

but still clearly there,
and staring through the door
when I looked for my car,

waved back, pulled out,
then quickly vanished
down an avenue of sycamores

where glassy flecks of sunlight
skittered through the leaves, falling
blindingly along the empty street.

Cuba

My eldest sister arrived home that morning
In her white muslin evening dress.
'Who the hell do you think you are,
Running out to dances in next to nothing?
As though we hadn't enough bother
With the world at war, if not at an end.'
My father was pounding the breakfast-table.

'Those Yankees were touch and go as it was –
If you'd heard Patton in Armagh –
But this Kennedy's nearly an Irishman
So he's not much better than ourselves.
And him with only to say the word.
If you've got anything on your mind
Maybe you should make your peace with God.'

I could hear May from beyond the curtain.
'Bless me, Father, for I have sinned.
I told a lie once, I was disobedient once.
And, Father, a boy touched me once.'
'Tell me, child. Was this touch immodest?
Did he touch your breast, for example?'
'He brushed against me, Father. Very gently.'

Why Brownlee Left

Why Brownlee left, and where he went,
Is a mystery even now.
For if a man should have been content
It was him; two acres of barley,
One of potatoes, four bullocks,
A milker, a slated farmhouse.
He was last seen going out to plough
On a March morning, bright and early.

By noon Brownlee was famous;
They had found all abandoned, with
The last rig unbroken, his pair of black
Horses, like man and wife,
Shifting their weight from foot to
Foot, and gazing into the future.

LESLIE NORRIS

A Glass Window

In Memory of Edward Thomas,
at Eastbury Church

The road lay in moistening valleys, lanes
Awash with evening, expensive racehorses
Put to bed in pastures under the elms.
I was disappointed. Something in me turns

Urchin at so much formality, such pastoral
Harmony. I grumble for rock outcrops,
In filed, rasping country. The church drips
Gently, in perfect English, and we all

Troop in, see the lit window, smile, and look
Again; shake out wet coats. Under your name
The images of village, hill and home,
And crystal England stands against the dark.

The path cut in the pane most worries me,
Coming from nowhere, moving into nowhere.
Is it the road to the land no traveller
Tells of? I turn away, knowing it is, for me,

That sullen lane leading you out of sight,
In darkening France, the road taken.
Suddenly I feel the known world shaken
By gunfire, by glass breaking. In comes the night.

Lear at Fifty

This morning early, driving the lanes in my
    Glib metal, frost fur on the brambles,
The grass, the hasps and bars of gates, first
    Sun burning it away in clinging wisps,

I saw an old man, sweeping leaves together, outside
    The Black Horse. His face held night's

Stupor, the lines of his age had not stiffened
    Against the daylight. He shifted his
Feet to careful standing, and then his broom,
    His necessary crutch, moved like an
Insect on slow, frail, crawling legs from
    Leaf to leaf. The small gusts of

My passing broke his labour, heaps of the dry
    Work spilling and flying. Nobody
Walked on the shore. Waves, unexpected heavy waves
    From some wild, piling storm away at sea,
Ripped the mild sand, smashed rocks, and shot the
    Squalling gulls out of the filth, vomit

And glittering sewage the flung birds flocked for,
    And truly, the tide was high this morning;
Old shoes, cans, cynical gouts of accidental oil,
    Plastic bottles, ropes, bubbling detergent
Slime, all were thrown to the sea wall. I have
    No wish to remember those unwelcoming

Waves I turned my back on, nor to think of old men
    Sitting tight in their skulls, aghast
At what their soft, insistent mouths will keep on
    Yelling. But through the limpet hours
I've walked the fields as if on a cliff's edge,
    The idea of flight in me, and seen my

Friends, myself, all strong, governing men, turned
    Sticks, turned tottering old fools.
The last sun in its blaze brings yellow light
    To everything, walls, windows, water;
A false warmth. In the morning some old man will start
    To sweep his leaves to a neatness.

162

JOHN ORMOND

My Grandfather and his Apple Tree

Life sometimes held such sweetness for him
As to engender guilt. From the night vein he'd come,
From working in water wrestling the coal,
Up the pit slant. Every morning hit him
Like a journey of trams between the eyes;
A wild and drinking farmboy sobered by love
Of a miller's daughter and a whitewashed cottage
Suddenly to pay rent for. So he'd left the farm
For dark under the fields six days a week
With mandrel and shovel and different stalls.
All light was beckoning. Soon his hands
Untangled a brown garden into neat greens.

There was an apple tree he limed, made sturdy;
The fruit was sweet and crisp upon the tongue
Until it budded temptation in his mouth.
Now he had given up whistling on Sundays,
Attended prayer-meetings, added a concordance
To his wedding Bible and ten children
To the village population. He nudged the line,
Clean-pinafored and collared, glazed with soap,
Every seventh day of rest in Ebenezer;
Shaved on a Saturday night to escape the devil.

The sweetness of the apples worried him.
He took a branch of cooker from a neighbour
When he became a deacon, wanting
The best of both his worlds. Clay from the colliery
He thumbed about the bole one afternoon
Grafting the sour to sweetness, bound up
The bleeding white of junction with broad strips
Of working flannel-shirt and belly-bands
To join the two in union. For a time
After the wound healed the sweetness held,
The balance tilted towards an old delight.

But in the time that I remember him
(His wife had long since died, I never saw her)
The sour half took over. Every single apple
Grew – across twenty Augusts – bitter as wormwood.
He'd sit under the box tree, his pink gums
(Between the white moustache and goatee beard)
Grinding thin slices that his jack-knife cut,
Sucking for sweetness vainly. It had gone,
Gone. I heard him mutter
Quiet Welsh oaths as he spat the gall-juice
Into the seeding onion-bed, watched him toss
The big core into the spreading nettles.

The Key

Its teeth worked doubtfully
At the worn wards of the lock,
Argued half-heartedly
With the lock's fixed dotage.
Between them they deferred decision.
One would persist, the other
Not relent. That lock and key
Were old when Linus Yale
Himself was born. Theirs
Was an ageless argument.

The key was as long as my hand,
The ring of it the size
Of a girl's bangle. The bit
Was inches square. A grandiose key
Fit for a castle, yet our terraced
House was two rooms up, two down;
Flung there by sullen pit-owners
In a spasm of petulance, discovering
That colliers could not live
On the bare Welsh mountain:

Like any other house in the domino
Row, except that our door

Was nearly always on the latch.
Most people just walked in, with
'Anybody home?' in greeting
To the kitchen. This room
Saw paths of generations cross;
This was the place to which we all came
Back to talk by the oven, on the white
Bench. This was the home patch.

And so, if we went out, we hid
The key – though the whole village
Knew where it was – under a stone
By the front door. We lifted up
The stone, deposited the key
Neatly into its own shape
In the damp earth. There, with liquid
Metal, we could have cast,
Using that master mould,
Another key, had we had need of it.

Sometimes we'd dip a sea-gull's
Feather in oil, corkscrew it
Far into the keyhole to ease
The acrimony there. The feather, askew
In the lock, would spray black
Droplets of oil on the threshold
And dandruff of feather-barb.
The deep armoreal stiffness, tensed
Against us, stayed. We'd put away
The oil, scrub down the front step.

The others have gone for the long
Night away. The evidence of grass
Re-growing insists on it. This time
I come back to dispose of what there is.
The knack's still with me. I plunge home
The key's great stem, insinuate
Something that was myself between
The two old litigants. The key

Engages and the bolt gives to me
Some walls enclosing furniture.

Cathedral Builders

They climbed on sketchy ladders towards God,
With winch and pulley hoisted hewn rock into heaven,
Inhabited sky with hammers, defied gravity,
Deified stone, took up God's house to meet Him,

And came down to their suppers and small beer;
Every night slept, lay with their smelly wives,
Quarrelled and cuffed the children, lied,
Spat, sang, were happy or unhappy,

And every day took to the ladders again;
Impeded the rights of way of another summer's
Swallows, grew greyer, shakier, became less inclined
To fix a neighbour's roof of a fine evening,

Saw naves sprout arches, clerestories soar,
Cursed the loud fancy glaziers for their luck,
Somehow escaped the plague, got rheumatism,
Decided it was time to give it up,

To leave the spire to others; stood in the crowd
Well back from the vestments at the consecration,
Envied the fat bishop his warm boots,
Cocked up a squint eye and said, 'I bloody did that.'

TOM PAULIN

Second-Rate Republics

The dull ripe smell of gas,
A pile of envelopes fading
On the hall table – no one
In this rented atmosphere remembers
The names who once gave this address.

We might be forgotten already,
She thinks, as she climbs the stairs
To spend a long weekend with him.
The trees in these brick avenues
Are showing full and green
Against the windows of partitioned rooms.
The air is humid, and down the street
She hears the single bark
Of a car door slamming shut.

He touches her and she sees herself
Being forced back into a shabby city
Somewhere else in Europe: how clammy
It is, how the crowds press and slacken
On the pavement, shaking photographs
Of a statesman's curdled face.

Now there is only a thin sheet
Between their struggling bodies
And the stained mattress.
Now his face hardens like a photograph,
And in the distance she hears
The forced jubilance of a crowd
That is desolate and obedient.

Pot Burial

He has married again. His wife
Buys ornaments and places them
On the dark sideboard. Year by year
Her vases and small jugs crowd out
The smiles of the wife who died.

PETER PORTER

From Three Poems for Music

Though this is not in Hesiod,
Music was stolen from a God:

Not fire but notes the primal giver
Paid for with helpings of his liver

And virtuosi of the earth
Outsang the Gods who gave them birth.

When Orpheus plays we meet Apollo,
When there's theology to swallow

We set it to music, our greatest art,
One that's both intellect *and* heart,

There war and peace alike depict us
(Drums and trumpets in the Benedictus) –

It sang beneath the Grecian boat,
It kept Pythagoras afloat,

It suffered poets, critics, chat
And will no doubt survive Darmstadt;

This brandy of the damned of course
To some is just a bottled sauce,

Its treasons, spoils and stratagems
Aleatory as women's hems

Yet beauty who indulged the swan
At death completes her with a song

And Paradise till we are there
Is in these measured lengths of air.

Mort aux Chats

There will be no more cats.
Cats spread infection,
cats pollute the air,
cats consume seven times
their own weight in food a week,
cats were worshipped in
decadent societies (Egypt
and Ancient Rome), the Greeks
had no use for cats. Cats
sit down to pee (our scientists
have proved it). The copulation
of cats is harrowing; they
are unbearably fond of the moon.
Perhaps they are all right in
their own country but their
traditions are alien to ours.
Cats smell, they can't help it,
you notice it going upstairs.
Cats watch too much television,
they can sleep through storms,
they stabbed us in the back
last time. There have never been
any great artists who were cats.
They don't deserve a capital C
except at the beginning of a sentence.
I blame my headache and my
plants dying on to cats.
Our district is full of them,
property values are falling.
When I dream of God I see
a Massacre of Cats. Why
should they insist on their own
language and religion, who

needs to purr to make his point?
Death to all cats! The Rule
of Dogs shall last a thousand years!

An Exequy

In wet May, in the months of change,
In a country you wouldn't visit, strange
Dreams pursue me in my sleep,
Black creatures of the upper deep –
Though you are five months dead, I see
You in guilt's iconography,
Dear Wife, lost beast, beleaguered child,
The stranded monster with the mild
Appearance, whom small waves tease,
(Andromeda upon her knees
In orthodox deliverance)
And you alone of pure substance,
The unformed form of life, the earth
Which Piero's brushes brought to birth
For all to greet as myth, a thing
Out of the box of imagining.

This introduction serves to sing
Your mortal death as Bishop King
Once hymned in tetrametric rhyme
His young wife, lost before her time;
Though he lived on for many years
His poem each day fed new tears
To that unreaching spot, her grave,
His lines a baroque architrave
The Sunday poor with bottled flowers
Would by-pass in their mourning hours,
Esteeming ragged natural life
('Most dearly loved, most gentle wife'),
Yet, looking back when at the gate
And seeing grief in formal state
Upon a sculpted angel group,

Were glad that men of god could stoop
To give the dead a public stance
And freeze them in their mortal dance.

The words and faces proper to
My misery are private – you
Would never share your heart with those
Whose only talent's to suppose,
Nor from your final childish bed
Raise a remote confessing head –
The channels of our lives are blocked,
The hand is stopped upon the clock,
No one can say why hearts will break
And marriages are all opaque:
A map of loss, some posted cards,
The living house reduced to shards,
The abstract hell of memory,
The pointlessness of poetry –
These are the instances which tell
Of something which I know full well,
I owe a death to you – one day
The time will come for me to pay
When your slim shape from photographs
Stands at my door and gently asks
If I have any work to do
Or will I come to bed with you.
O scala enigmatica,
I'll climb up to that attic where
The curtain of your life was drawn
Some time between despair and dawn –
I'll never know with what halt steps
You mounted to this plain eclipse
But each stair now will station me
A black responsibility
And point me to that shut-down room,
'This be your due appointed tomb.'

I think of us in Italy:
Gin-and-chianti-fuelled, we

Move in a trance through Paradise,
Feeding at last our starving eyes,
Two people of the English blindness
Doing each masterpiece the kindness
Of discovering it – from Baldovinetti
To Venice's most obscure jetty.
A true unfortunate traveller, I
Depend upon your nurse's eye
To pick the altars where no Grinner
Puts us off our tourists' dinner
And in hotels to bandy words
With Genevan girls and talking birds,
To wear your feet out following me
To night's end and true amity,
And call my rational fear of flying
A paradigm of Holy Dying –
And, oh my love, I wish you were
Once more with me, at night somewhere
In narrow streets applauding wines,
The moon above the Apennines
As large as logic and the stars,
Most middle-aged of avatars,
As bright as when they shone for truth
Upon untried and avid youth.

The rooms and days we wandered through
Shrink in my mind to one – there you
Lie quite absorbed by peace – the calm
Which life could not provide is balm
In death. Unseen by me, you look
Past bed and stairs and half-read book
Eternally upon your home,
The end of pain, the left alone.
I have no friend, or intercessor,
No psychopomp or true confessor
But only you who know my heart
In every cramped and devious part –
Then take my hand and lead me out,
The sky is overcast by doubt,

The time has come, I listen for
Your words of comfort at the door,
O guide me through the shoals of fear –
'Fürchte dich nicht, ich bin bei dir.'

Non Piangere, Liù

A card comes to tell you
you should report
to have your eyes tested.

But your eyes melted in the fire
and the only tears, which soon dried,
fell in the chapel.

Other things still come –
invoices, subscription renewals,
shiny plastic cards promising credit –
not much for a life spent
in the service of reality.

You need answer none of them.
Nor my asking you for one drop
of succour in my own hell.

Do not cry, I tell myself,
the whole thing is a comedy
and comedies end happily.

The fire will come out of the sun
and I shall look in the heart of it.

TOM POW

Invitation

Step through
the ragged hawthorn
into the park:
by a frozen pond
a muffled toddler
has absconded.
See her make
a clockwork run
at a scattering fan
of silver birds –
her open arms raised
in a gesture
of hopeless desire.

SHEENAGH PUGH

'Do you think we'll ever get to see Earth, sir?'

I hear they're hoping to run trips
one day, for the young and fit, of course.
I don't see much use in it myself;
there'll be any number of places
you can't land, because they're still toxic,
and even in the relatively safe bits
you won't see what it was; what it could be.
I can't fancy a tour through the ruins
of my home with a party of twenty-five
and a guide to tell me what to see.
But if you should see some beautiful thing,
some leaf, say, damascened with frost,
some iridescence on a pigeon's neck,
some stone, some curve, some clear water;
look at it as if you were made of eyes,
as if you were nothing but an eye, lidless
and tender, to be probed and scorched
by extreme light. Look at it with your skin,
with the small hairs on the back of your neck.
If it is well-shaped, look at it with your hands;
if it has fragrance, breathe it into yourself;
if it tastes sweet, put your tongue to it.
Look at it as a happening, a moment;
let nothing of it go unrecorded,
map it as if it were already passing.
Look at it with the inside of your head,
look at it for later, look at it for ever,
and look at it once for me.

The Frozen Field

I saw a flat space
by a river: from the air
a jigsaw-piece. It is green
by times, and brown, and golden,
and white. When green, it gives food
to animals: when golden,
to men. Brown, it is ridged
and patterned, but when white,
a plane of evenness.

When frost touches it by night,
it turns silver: blue shadows
etch the hollows, grassblades glitter
in the grip of silence. It was
in such a place as this,
elsewhere, on the coldest night
of a cold winter, two boys
drove a car, with some difficulty,
over the frozen hummocks: parked
in the breathtaking chill, the stillness
that weighed each leaf down,
and shot each other.

It was a place I knew
years ago: I must have seen
the field, in summer maybe,
growing turnips, grazing cattle,
dotted with the white
of sheep, the blue and orange
of tents, and all the time
travelling toward one night
vast with misery; the sharp cracks,
one-two, like branches in frost,
that broke the silence.

Who knows what a field
has seen? Maldon sounds
of marsh birds, boats, the east wind.
The thin wail across the mudflats
is a heron or a gull, not Wulfmaer,
the boy who chose to die
with his king, never having guessed
how long dying could take.

And an oak lives
a long time, but a nail-hole
soon closes. Of all the oaks
at Clontarf, which is the one
where Ulf Hreda nailed one end
of a man's guts, and walked him
round and round the tree, unwinding
at every step?

The night the boys died,
their field was Maldon was Clontarf,
was Arbela, Sedgemoor, Solferino,
was every field where a moon
has risen on grass stiff
with blood, on silvered faces.
. . . Aughrim was so white,
they said, with young bones,
it would never need lime again:
better not to see
in the mind's eye Magenta,
that named a new dye.

It was as if the field
clenched all this in
on itself, hunched over
the pain of all young men
since time began; as if
every crop it ever bore
crowded in on it: barley, blood,

sheep, leisure, suicide,
sorrow, so much, its being
could not stay in bounds
but spilled out over space
and time, unwinding
meanings as it went.

They tangle around
the field's riddle now: *I saw a stage*
for pain, a suffering-space.
The fine mist of aloneness closed it
in the morning: at sunset
it was flooded with blood.

Thinking such things often,
we should see too much. I see
a picnic place, a playground.
My eyes half-open, I lean
against a tree; hear through the ground
children's feet chasing.
The sunlight shivers: *someone*
walked over my grave. I chew
on a stiff grassblade.

The Behaviour of Dogs

Their feet are four-leafed clovers
that leave a jigsaw in the dust.

They grin like Yale keys and tease
us with joke-shop Niagara tongues.

A whippet jack-knifes across the grass
to where the afghan's palomino fringe

is part Opera House curtain, part
Wild Bill Hicock. Its head

precedes the rest, balanced like
a tray, aloft and to the left.

The labrador cranks a village pump,
the boxer shimmies her rump,

docked to a door knocker, and
the alsation rattles a sabre –

only the ones with crewcuts fight.
Sportif, they scratch their itches

like one-legged cyclists sprinting
for home, pee like hurdlers,

shit like weightlifters, and relax
by giving each other piggy backs . . .

Flying to Belfast, 1977

It was possible to laugh
as the engines whistled to the boil,

and wonder what the clouds looked like –
shovelled snow, Apple Charlotte,

Tufty Tails . . . I enjoyed
the Irish Sea, the ships were faults

in a dark expanse of linen.
And then Belfast below, a radio

with its back ripped off,
among the agricultural abstract

of the fields. Intricate,
neat and orderly. The windows

gleamed like drops of solder –
everything was wired up.

I thought of wedding presents,
white tea things

grouped on a dresser,
as we entered the cloud

and were nowhere –
a bride in a veil, laughing

at the sense of event, only
half afraid of an empty house

with its curtains boiling
from the bedroom window.

A Martian Sends a Postcard Home

Caxtons are mechanical birds with many wings
and some are treasured for their markings –

they cause the eyes to melt
or the body to shriek without pain.

I have never seen one fly, but
sometimes they perch on the hand.

Mist is when the sky is tired of flight
and rests its soft machine on ground:

then the world is dim and bookish
like engravings under tissue paper.

Rain is when the earth is television.
It has the property of making colours darker.

Model T is a room with the lock inside –
a key is turned to free the world

for movement, so quick there is a film
to watch for anything missed.

But time is tied to the wrist
or kept in a box, ticking with impatience.

In homes, a haunted apparatus sleeps,
that snores when you pick it up.

If the ghost cries, they carry it
to their lips and soothe it to sleep

with sounds. And yet, they wake it up
deliberately, by tickling with a finger.

Only the young are allowed to suffer
openly. Adults go to a punishment room

with water but nothing to eat.
They lock the door and suffer the noises

alone. No one is exempt
and everyone's pain has a different smell.

At night, when all the colours die,
they hide in pairs

and read about themselves –
in colour, with their eyelids shut.

PETER REDGROVE

On the Patio

A wineglass overflowing with thunderwater
Stands out on the drumming steel table

Among the outcries of the downpour
Feathering chairs and rethundering on the awnings.

How the pellets of water shooting miles
Fly into the glass of swirl, and slop

Over the table's scales of rust
Shining like chained sores,

Because the rain eats everything except the glass
Of spinning water that is clear down here

But purple with rumbling depths above, and this cloud
Is transferring its might into a glass

In which thunder and lightning come to rest,
The cloud crushed into a glass.

Suddenly I dart out into the patio,
Snatch the bright glass up and drain it,

Bang it back down on the thundery steel table for a
refill.

Orchard with Wasps

The rouged fruits in
The orchard by the waterfall, the bronzed fruits,

The brassy flush on the apples.
He gripped the fruit

184

And it buzzed like a gong stilled with his fingers
And a wasp flew out with its note

From the gong of sugar and scented rain
All the gongs shining like big rain under the trees

Within the sound of the little waterfall
Like a gash in the apple-flesh of time

Streaming with its juices and bruised.
Such a wasp, so full of sugar

Flew out within the sound
Of the apple-scented waterfall,

Such a gondola of yellow rooms
Striped with black rooms

Fuelled with syrups hovering
At the point of crystal,

Applegenius, loverwasp, scimitar
Of scented air and sugar-energy

Shining up his lamp-tree tall and devious
Given utterly to its transformations

From sharp-scented flowers to honey-gongs,
Giver and taker of pollination-favours,

A small price for such syrups and plunderings,
Its barky flesh, its beckoning fruit,

Its deep odour of cider and withering grasses,
Its brassy bottles and its Aladdin gold-black drunks.

A Scarecrow

A scarecrow in the field,
Dressed like a King
In streamers of tinfoil
Which flash in the sun
And glitter;

And in the deep night
As the moon rises
That glittering again
Appears in the field
As if a fountain
Were standing guard
Over the furrows;

A tattering robe
Of strips of tinfoil
Ragged and gorgeous because
Of its liquid facility with the light,
And so multiplex

That it is a squadron riding
With swords out saluting the light.

The birds rejoice with their song
At this wonder of the sun
Willowing on its cross-pole,
And in this presence of the moon
Raggedy in the fertile field,
And nip therefore their share only
Of seeds sown out of the loam,
And do not multiply their kind
Desperately being content seemingly
That an alchemical balance has been achieved:

The tinfoil rebus in the open field.
Even the vicar, passing the scarecrow field
Is reminded of life

That is not only dust to dust
But light to light and air to air,
Shooting his cuffs,
Flashing his watch.

Entry Fee

When I stroke her arms
There is a smell of bread;
Her legs, of lilies.

There are fragrant marshes in her skin
And there is a pulse in the ground of it.
The Mine called 'Isyours' is open today
On payment of a small compliment.

This is really
Very extraordinary value;
The lights are blazing underground,
Gemstone studs the walls and floors;
I walk there amazed for hours, it seems.

At the very bottom of the shaft
There is a dark pool with a white swan floating

It rouses its wings

It beats over the water
Pleating it to its depths
Raising a new odour charged
With the deep and with the extreme
Cry of the bird as it ladders across the pool.

JEREMY REED

Tulips

These have the reticence of pedigree
breeding, an overstrained, suave dignity

that keeps a poker-grip on things; a tight
refusal to open out to the light,

adamant, in their baronial excess
of colour, torch-bearers under duress

to hold their cool composure for three weeks
in strains of scarlet, mauve, crimson with streaks

of gold, flaming tangerine and dove-white.
Their haughtiness is nerves; each scion's fright

is premature collapse, the palsied shake
that starts a tulip's death; the centre breaks

to reveal a shell crater; each petal
resisting a quick coronary fall,

leaves six blackened candle-wicks as stamen –
a burnt out candelabra on a stem . . .

Tagged with insignias, Abbu Hassan,
Cape Cod, Dragon Light, they resist the rain,

immaculate, close-ranked, a furnace glare
of colour maintained with their special flare

to avoid thought of their future decline,
goblets revealing on both sides the wine

of their rich fermentation, while the bee's
their gold-striped headdress and emissary.

Buoys

Punch drunk are worked over,
beleaguered by each sea's
top-spin of swell, lathered
and pitched to queasily

restabilize, they are ochre
pumpkin-heads pocked with rust shale
in a whorl of white water,
grouting like snouts in a pail

in the momentary backwash
of Atlantic welter.
To seagulls they're atolls,
to the tern flying saucers,

and obesely unsinkable,
they are a boxer's nightmare
of a face repeatedly hit
that won't black-out, but stays there.

They are bulk opposing a sea
that never stops running, markers
of dangerous shoals, their bells
warning off intruders

gruffly as farm-dogs. Herded
out across nautical charts,
they are inshore satellites,
playing their rumbustious parts

for all sea-craft. Vigilant bulls
confined to marking time,

they too in their anchorage
tug at a nose-chain,

and snore hoarsely in storm,
the sea waterbug-green,
beneath a sky black
as a cormorant's sheen.

Two I see wintering
at grass in a shipping yard,
veterans of long wars,
their grizzled tonsures hard

with resilience, awaiting
new paint, their cyclopean
eyeballs gone rusty from staring
unlidded at the ocean.

ALASTAIR REID

The O-Filler

One noon in the library, I watched a man –
imagine! – filling in O's, a little, rumpled
nobody of a man, who licked his stub of pencil
and leaned over every O with a loving care,
shading it neatly, exactly to its edges
until the open pages
were pocked and dotted with solid O's, like towns
and capitals on a map. And yet, so peppered,
the book appeared inhabited and complete.

That whole afternoon, as the light outside softened
and the library groaned woodenly,
he worked and worked, his o-so-patient shading
descending like an eyelid over each open O
for page after page. Not once did he miss one,
or hover even a moment over an *a*
or an *e* or a *p* or a *g*. Only the O's –
oodles of O's, O's multitudinous, O's manifold,
O's italic and roman.
And what light on his crumpled face when he
                                discovered –
as I supposed – odd words like *zoo* and *ooze*,
polo, *oolong* and *odontology*!

Think now. In that limitless library,
all round the steep-shelved walls, bulging in their
                                bindings,
books stood, waiting. Heaven knows how many
he had so far filled, but still there remained
uncountable volumes of O-laden prose, and odes
with inflated capital O's (in the manner of Shelley),
O-bearing Bibles and biographies,
even whole sections devoted to O alone,
all his for the filling. Glory, glory, glory!

How utterly open and endless the world must have
                              seemed to him,
how round and ample! Think of it. A pencil
was all he needed. Life was one wide O.

And why, at the end of things, should O's not be closed
as eyes are? I envied him, for in my place
across the table from him, had I accomplished
anything as firm as he had, or as fruitful?
What could I show? A handful of scrawled lines,
an afternoon yawned and wondered away,
and a growing realisation that in time
even my scribbled words would come
under his grubby thumb, and the blinds be drawn
on all my O's, with only this thought for comfort –
that when he comes to this poem, a proper joy
may amaze his wizened face and, o, a pure pleasure
make his meticulous pencil quiver.

A Lesson in Music

Play the tune again: but this time
with more regard for the movement at the source of it
and less attention to time. Time falls
curiously in the course of it.

Play the tune again: not watching
your fingering, but forgetting, letting flow
the sound till it surrounds you. Do not count
or even think. Let go.

Play the tune again: but try to be
nobody, nothing, as though the pace
of the sound were your heart beating, as though
the music were your face.

Play the tune again. It should be easier
to think less every time of the notes, of the measure.

It is all an arrangement of silence. Be silent, and then
play it for your pleasure.

Play the tune again; and this time, when it ends,
do not ask me what I think. Feel what is happening
strangely in the room as the sound glooms over
you, me, everything.

Now,
play the tune again.

CHRISTOPHER REID

Big Ideas with Loose Connections

These monumental Hs must have dropped here
from some heavenly alphabet.

Upright at opposite ends of a turbulent field,
they point woodenly in the direction of hope.

Giants, the epigones of Uranus,
stamp around in the cold, steaming like cattle.

Their lives are ruled by improbable fictions:
lines, flags and whistles;

a thirty-two-legged spider that wheels and buckles
over the agony of its stubborn leather egg.

From a gusty somewhere, God looks down on a world
perfectly simple. We are in love.

The giants are having fun.
Nearby, a blind man tickles the pathway,

whose white stick marks a cardiogram,
no-one but he can follow.

A wriggling, long-tailed kite leaps like a sperm
at the sun, its blurry ovum.

A Tune

Stammered on a mandolin,
an old sentimental tune
from an open doorway in summer:
of course, it's only a radio thinking aloud

194

and nobody paying much attention.
Who can afford to lose tears over music these days?

I have heard the same song
in numerous clever disguises –
embellished with hesitations and surprise chords
by my cousin, the promising fiddler;
crooned almost silently by women in kitchens
to lull children or coax the rising of the dough.

And then there was the dance band
that came twice a year to our village.
My father explained the workings of the bass tuba,
how the breath was obliged to travel patiently
through those shiny intestines, before it could issue
in a sound halfway between serious and rude.

Its thoughtful flatulence underscored
both the quick dances, and the slow ones
where the men took the women in their proprietorial
                                    embrace
and moved about the floor with an ostentatious
                                    dreaminess.
The band played an arrangement of the very tune
that someone's radio is remembering right now.

I dare say it means something to you as well.
Amazing, how a piece of nonsense like this can survive,
more obstinate than any national anthem.
Perhaps they will dig it out again for my funeral:
a six-piece band ought to be sufficient,
with wind, an accordion, drums and at least one
                              ceremonious tuba.

OLIVER REYNOLDS

Thaw

It was a pure world, snow-covered.

I was working on an algebraic model
of the long fall, almost aleatory, of flakes
intersected by slicing and sweeping gulls
when the phone rang:

the Radio Committee boss going bazurkas
because the Friend of Children had tuned into
Yudina playing the Mozart 23rd
and wanted the record of it.
Who was the boss to say it was a live broadcast?
If the Great Gardener thought it was a record,
it was a record: if Stalin said shit,
you shat.

So off they went to Archives to find
Yudina had never recorded the 23rd.
We had to do it then. That night.

The studio was frigid bedlam;
the tympanist was still in his pyjamas,
the woodwind had no scores
so, out of habit, were falling back on the '1812'
while the conductor was so nervous
his adagio kept twitching into allegro.

Yudina was the only calm one;
when I swore at a fuse blowing she said
'You're far from God, you must be closer to God.'

We made the pressing at daybreak: just one copy.
Three of us took it over to Dispatch
like a bomb disposal squad with Parkinson's.

Snow huffed and puffed at us all the way;
it was 16 below and we were sweating.
Carrying it, I felt limp and giggly;
I remembered the Latin *effetus*:
weakened by having brought forth young.

That record was on the turntable in his dacha
when the Great Railway Engineer finally died:
the music at an end, allegro assai,
whirling outer air configured with flakes
and the still pause inside tightening
at 78 revolutions a minute
scrik . . . scrik . . . scrik . . . scrik . . .

ALAN ROSS

Stanley Matthews

Not often *con brio*, but *andante*, *andante*,
    horseless, though jockey-like and jaunty,
Straddling the touchline, live margin
    not out of the game, nor quite in,
Made by him green and magnetic, stroller
Indifferent as a cat dissembling, rolling
A little as on deck, till the mouse, the ball,
    slides palely to him,
And shyly almost, with deprecatory cough, he is off.

Head of a Perugino, with faint flare
Of the nostrils, as though Lipizzaner-like,
    he sniffed at the air,
Finding it good beneath him, he draws
Defenders towards him, the ball a bait
They refuse like a poisoned chocolate,
    retreating, till he slows his gait
To a walk, inviting the tackle, inciting it.

Till, unrefusable, dangling the ball at the instep,
He is charged – and stiffening so slowly
It is barely perceptible, he executes with a squirm
Of the hips, a twist more suggestive than apparent,
    that lazily disdainful move *toreros* term
        a Veronica – it's enough.
Only emptiness following him, pursuing some scent
Of his own, he weaves in towards,
    not away from, fresh tacklers,
Who, turning about to gain time, are by him
    harried, pursued not pursuers.

Now gathers speed, nursing the ball as he cruises,
Eyes judging distance, noting the gaps, the spaces
Vital for colleagues to move to, slowing a trace,

198

As from Vivaldi to Dibdin, pausing,
   and leisurely, leisurely, swings
To the left upright his centre, on hips
His hands, observing the goalkeeper spring,
   heads rising vainly to the ball's curve
Just as it's plucked from them; and dispassionately
Back to his mark he trots, whistling through closed lips.

Trim as a yacht, with similar lightness
   – of keel, of reaction to surface – with salt air
Tanned, this incomparable player, in decline fair
   to look at, nor in decline either,
Improving like wine with age, has come far –
   born to one, a barber, who boxed,
Not with such filial magnificence, but well.
'The greatest of all time,' *meraviglioso* Matthews –
   Stoke City, Blackpool and England.
Expressionless enchanter, weaving as on strings
Conceptual patterns to a private music, heard
Only by him, to whose slowly emerging theme
He rehearses steps, soloist in compulsions of a dream.

CAROL RUMENS

Seroyeshky

We broke slim boughs to stir
and sift the leaf-mould.

I was befogged by earth-colours,
my earth-bound sight an Axminster

of swirling oakleaves, beech-mast,
till I had trimmed my focus

to detail, even acquired
a touch of your magical foresight.

Seroyeshky, you called them:
mushrooms for eating raw,

but better cooked, you said,
in spite of the nickname.

Some were pale red, some amber;
the slugs had frilled their edges

and nipped small coins from them:
still, they were beautiful,

thrusting up stoutly,
bursting the thatch of their caves,

and yet most breakable,
their spore-weight slight as grass.

The Pinner woods were glowing
in a Muscovite sunset

as we brought home our catch.
You cleaned them and fried them

to a milky gloss;
eagerly we dipped our forks.

The bitterness was astounding.
We've been warned, I said.

Whatever else they look like,
whatever they are, elsewhere,

here, they are toadstools,
here, our enemies.

And so we abandoned them
– our prized seroyeshky, love-sick

fantasies of tasting
the past, or another's country.

CAROLE SATYAMURTI

Broken Moon
for Emma

Twelve, small as six,
strength, movement, hearing
all given in half measure,
my daughter,
child of genetic carelessness,
walks uphill, always.

I watch her morning face;
precocious patience as she hooks each sock,
creeps it up her foot,
aims her jersey like a quoit.
My fingers twitch;
her private frown deters.

Her jokes can sting:
'My life is like dressed crab
– lot of effort, rather little meat.'
Yet she delights in seedlings taking root,
finding a fossil,
a surprise dessert.

Chopin will not yield to her stiff touch;
I hear her cursing.
She paces Bach exactly,
firm rounding of perfect cadences.
Somewhere inside
she is dancing a courante.

In dreams she skims the sand,
curls toes into the ooze of pools,
leaps on to stanchions.
Awake, her cousins take her hands;
they lean into the waves,
stick-child between curved sturdiness.

She turns away from stares,
laughs at the boy who asks
if she will find a midget husband.
Ten years ago, cradling her,
I showed her the slice of silver in the sky.
'Moon broken,' she said.

Mouthfuls

They lasted longer then.
Mars Bar paper crackled
as we rewrapped half for later,
sliced the rest
to thin cross-sections,
arranged them like wedding-cake
– loaves and fishes.

Sherbet lemons, hard against the palate,
vicious yellow. Strong sucking
made them spurt, fizz, foam,
sugar splinters lacerate
the inside of my cheeks,
surprising as ice crystals in the wind
that cut my legs through socks.

Licorice comfits shaken in a tin
made marching music.
Or they were fairy food
– each colour wrought a different magic:
mauve for shrinking,
green, the power to fly,
red, the brightest, eternal sleep.

The oddity of gob-stoppers:
tonguing each detail
of the surface – porcelain,
tiny roughnesses,
licking, rolling it, recapturing

the grain and silk of nipple;
rainbows glimpsed only in mirrors.

A shorter life for jelly babies
– drafted into armies, black ones last,
or wrapped in paper shawls in matchbox beds,
taken out, chewed from the feet up,
decapitated out of kindness
or, squeamishly sucked,
reduced to embryos.

VERNON SCANNELL

Taken in Adultery

Shadowed by shades and spied upon by glass
Their search for privacy conducts them here,
With an irony that neither notices,
To a public house; the wrong time of the year
For outdoor games; where, over gin and tonic,
Best bitter and potato crisps, they talk
Without much zest, almost laconic,
Flipping an occasional remark.
Would you guess that they were lovers, this dull pair?
The answer, I suppose, is yes, you would.
Despite her spectacles and faded hair
And his worn look of being someone's Dad
You know that they are having an affair
And neither finds it doing them much good.
Presumably, in one another's eyes,
They must look different from what we see,
Desirable in some way, otherwise
They'd hardly choose to come here, furtively,
And mutter their bleak needs above the mess
Of fag-ends, crumpled cellophane and crumbs,
Their love-feast's litter. Though they might profess
To find great joy together, all that comes
Across to us is tiredness, melancholy.
When they are silent each seems listening;
There must be many voices in the air:
Reproaches, accusations, suffering
That no amount of passion keeps elsewhere.
Imperatives that brought them to this room,
Stiff from the car's back seat, lose urgency;
They start to wonder who's betraying whom,
How it will end, and how did it begin –
The woman taken in adultery
And the man who feels he, too, was taken in.

No Sense of Direction

I have always admired
Those who are sure
Which turning to take,
Who need no guide
Even in war
When thunders shake
The torn terrain,
When battalions of shrill
Stars all desert
And the derelict moon
Goes over the hill:
Eyes chained by the night
They find their way back
As if it were daylight.
Then, on peaceful walks
Over strange wooded ground,
They will find the right track,
Know which of the forks
Will lead to the inn
I would never have found;
For I lack their gift,
Possess almost no
Sense of direction.
And yet I owe
A debt to this lack,
A debt so vast
No reparation
Can ever be made,
For it led me away
From the road I sought
Which would carry me to –
I mistakenly thought –
My true destination:
It made me stray
To this lucky path
That ran like a fuse
And brought me to you

And love's bright, soundless
Detonation.

I'm Covered Now

'What would happen to your lady wife
And little ones – you've four I think you said –
Little ones I mean, not wives, ha-ha –
What would happen to them if . . .' And here
He cleared his throat of any reticence.
'. . . if something happened to you? We've got to face
These things, must be realistic, don't you think?
Now, we have various schemes to give you cover
And, taking in account your age and means,
This policy would seem to be the one . . .'

The words uncoiled, effortless but urgent,
Assured, yet coming just a bit too fast,
A little breathless, despite the ease of manner,
An athlete drawing near the tape's last gasp
Yet trying hard to seem still vigorous there.
But no, this metaphor has too much muscle;
His was an indoor art and every phrase
Was handled with a trained seducer's care.
I took the words to heart, or, if not heart,
Some region underneath intelligence,
The area where the hot romantic aria
And certain kinds of poetry are received.
And this Giovanni of the fast buck knew
My humming brain was pleasurably numb;
My limbs were weakening; he would soon achieve
The now explicit ends for which he'd come.
At last I nodded, glazed, and said I'd sign,
But he showed little proper satisfaction.
He sighed and sounded almost disappointed,
And I remembered hearing someone say
No Juan really likes an easy lay.
But I'll say this: he covered up quite quickly

And seemed almost as ardent as before
When he pressed my hand and said that he was happy
And hoped that I was, too.
                              And then the door
Was closed behind him as our deal was closed.
If something happened I was covered now.
Odd that I felt so chilly, so exposed.

Collected Poems Recollected
(for Peter Porter)

Most of us have smiled to see them there
On market stalls, at jumble sales, in rows
On dainty shelves in twilit bookshops, where
Mild yet vulturine explorers nose
Wheezily through seventeenth-century prose
And cough and chumble in that studious air.

Rarely disturbed, these Poets stand in line,
Quaint wall-flowers few will ever ask to dance
And none invite to share good food and wine;
Though you or I might flick a friendly glance
Most look at them, if look they do, askance,
In ways to chill the bibliological spine.

You, Peter, I am confident, could reel
Their names off, get them smartly on parade –
John Greenleaf Whittier (his three names peal
More plangently than any poem he made);
John Drinkwater (his verse, pale lemonade,
May disintoxicate but scarcely heal).

The Manxman, T. E. Brown (his shut leaves hide
Stuffed blackbird in a cardboard garden), stout
Noble, Bulwer Lytton, side by side
With fair Felicia Hemans; close about
Stand Gawsworth (next to *Ditties of a Scout*),
Great Noyes and Newbolt, monitors to Pride.

208

More female poets: Dora Sigerson Shorter,
And Edith Sitwell still failing to impress –
Posterity, as critic, yields no quarter –
Dark waiting spaces, especially under 'S' –
Surely for Spender? . . . Silkin? . . . Please say 'Yes'!
But none for Martial artist, Peter Porter.

For twenty years I've felt your poems were meant
For private shelves at home and in the mind.
The awkward squad, the not quite excellent
Earn, all the same, some homage of a kind:
Who knows for sure where he will be consigned?
Those foothills prove the peaks magnificent.

JON SILKIN

Death of a Son

(*who died in a mental hospital aged one*)

Something has ceased to come along with me.
Something like a person: something very like one.
And there was no nobility in it
Or anything like that.

Something was there like a one year
Old house, dumb as stone. While the near buildings
Sang like birds and laughed
Understanding the pact

They were to have with silence. But he
Neither sang nor laughed. He did not bless silence
Like bread, with words.
He did not forsake silence.

But rather, like a house in mourning
Kept the eye turned in to watch the silence while
The other houses like birds
Sang around him.

And the breathing silence neither
Moved nor was still.

I have seen stones: I have seen brick
But this house was made up of neither bricks nor stone
But a house of flesh and blood
With flesh of stone

And bricks for blood. A house
Of stones and blood in breathing silence with the other
Birds singing crazy on its chimneys.
But this was silence,

This was something else, this was
Hearing and speaking though he was a house drawn
    Into silence, this was
        Something religious in his silence,

    Something shining in his quiet,
This was different this was altogether something else:
    Though he never spoke, this
        Was something to do with death.

    And then slowly the eye stopped looking
Inward. The silence rose and became still.
The look turned to the outer place and stopped,
    With the birds still shrilling around him.
        And as if he could speak

He turned over on his side with his one year
Red as a wound
He turned over as if he could be sorry for this
And out of his eyes two great tears rolled, like stones,
                                    and he died.

A Daisy

Look unoriginal
Being numerous. They ask for attention
With that gradated yellow swelling
Of oily stamens. Petals focus them:
The eye-lashes grow wide.
Why should not one bring these to a funeral?
And at night, like children,
Without anxiety, their consciousness
Shut with white petals;

Blithe, individual.

The unwearying, small sunflower
Fills the grass

With versions of one eye.
A strength in the full look
Candid, solid, glad.
Domestic as milk.

In multitudes, wait,
Each, to be looked at, spoken to.
They do not wither;
Their going, a pressure
Of elate sympathy
Released from you.
Rich up to the last interval
With minute tubes of oil, pollen;
Utterly without scent, for the eye,
For the eye, simply. For the mind
And its invisible organ,
That feeling thing.

JAMES SIMMONS

Claudy
for Harry Barton

(*song*)

The Sperrins surround it, the Faughan flows by,
at each end of Main Street the hills and the sky,
the small town of Claudy at ease in the sun
last July in the morning, a new day begun.

How peaceful and pretty if the moment could stop,
McIlhenny is straightening things in his shop,
and his wife is outside serving petrol, and then
a girl takes a cloth to a big window pane.

And McCloskey is taking the weight off his feet,
and McClelland and Miller are sweeping the street,
and, delivering milk at the Beaufort Hotel,
young Temple's enjoying his first job quite well.

And Mrs McLaughlin is scrubbing her floor,
and Artie Hone's crossing the street to a door,
and Mrs Brown, looking around for her cat,
goes off up an entry – what's strange about that?

Not much – but before she comes back to the road
that strange car parked outside her house will explode,
and all of the people I've mentioned outside
will be waiting to die or already have died.

An explosion too loud for your ear drums to bear,
and young children squealing like pigs in the square,
and all faces chalk white and streaked with bright red,
and the glass and the dust and the terrible dead.

For an old lady's legs are ripped off, and the head
of a man's hanging open, and still he's not dead.

He is screaming for mercy, and his son stands and
                                                   stares
and stares, and then suddenly, quick, disappears.

And Christ, little Katharine Aikin is dead,
and Mrs McLaughlin is pierced through the head.
Meanwhile to Dungiven the killers have gone,
and they're finding it hard to get through on the phone.

C. H. SISSON

In Allusion to Propertius, I, iii

When I opened the door she was asleep.
It is thus I imagine the scene, after Propertius.

The torches flickered all over the world
My legs staggered but I went to her bed

And let myself down gently beside her.
Her head was propped lightly upon her hands.

I passed one arm under her body
And with my free hand I arranged her hair

Not disturbing her sleep. She was Ariadne
Desolate upon the coast where Theseus had left her,

Andromeda, no longer chained to the rock,
In her first sleep. Or she was Io,

A milk-white heifer browsing upon her dreams,
I Argus, watching her with my hundred eyes.

I took kisses from her and drew my sword.
Then, through the open window the moon looked in:

It was the white rays opened her eyes.
I expected her to reproach me, and she did:

Why had I not come to her bed before?
I explained that I lived in the underworld

Among shadows. She had been in that forest.
Had we not met, she said, in that place?

Hand in hand we wandered among the tree-trunks
And came into the light at the edge of the forest.

The Herb-Garden

When a stream ran across my path,
I stopped, dazzled, though the sparkle was at my feet;
The blind head moving forward, Gulliver
Walking toweringly over the little people.

Not that smaller in size meant, in any way, lesser;
It was merely that I could not see them, my eyes
Crunched on them as if they had been pebbles,
And I blundering without understanding.

Large is inept: how my loping arms fall,
The hands not prehensile, perpendicular
Before an inclined trunk. The legs do the damage,
Like the will of God without rhyme or reason.

Epithalamia are dreamed in this atmosphere
Which towers like a blue fastness over my head.
My head is full of rumours, but the perceptions
Dry like lavender within my skull.

Herb-garden, dream, scent of rosemary,
Scent of thyme, the deep error of sage,
Fennel that falls like a fountain, rue that says nothing,
Blue leaves, in a garden of green.

IAIN CRICHTON SMITH

Old Woman

And she, being old, fed from a mashed plate
as an old mare might droop across a fence
to the dull pastures of its ignorance.
Her husband held her upright while he prayed

to God who is all-forgiving to send down
some angel somewhere who might land perhaps
in his foreign wings among the gradual crops.
She munched, half dead, blindly searching the spoon.

Outside, the grass was raging. There I sat
imprisoned in my pity and my shame
that men and women having suffered time
should sit in such a place, in such a state

and wished to be away, yes, to be far away
with athletes, heroes, Greeks or Roman men
who pushed their bitter spears into a vein
and would not spend an hour with such decay.

'Pray God,' he said, 'we ask you, God,' he said.
The bowed back was quiet. I saw the teeth
tighten their grip around a delicate death.
And nothing moved within the knotted head

but only a few poor veins as one might see
vague wishless seaweed floating on a tide
of all the salty waters where had died
too many waves to mark two more or three.

Two Girls Singing

It neither was the words nor yet the tune.
Any tune would have done and any words.
Any listener or no listener at all.

As nightingales in rocks or a child crooning
in its own world of strange awakening
or larks for no reason but themselves.

So on the bus through late November running
by yellow lights tormented, darkness falling,
the two girls sang for miles and miles together

and it wasn't the words or tune. It was the singing.
It was the human sweetness in that yellow,
the unpredicted voices of our kind.

By Ferry to the Island

We crossed by ferry to the bare island
where sheep and cows stared coldly through the
                                                    wind –
the sea behind us with its silver water,
the silent ferryman standing in the stern
clutching his coat about him like old iron.

We landed from the ferry and went inland
past a small church down to the winding shore
where a white seagull fallen from the failing
chill and ancient daylight lay so pure
and softly breasted that it made more dear

the lesser white around us. There we sat,
sheltered by a rock beside the sea.
Someone made coffee, someone played the fool
in a high rising voice for two hours.
The sea's language was more grave and harsh.

218

And one sat there whose dress was white and cool.
The fool sparkled his wit that she might hear
new diamonds turning on her naked finger.
What might the sea think or the dull sheep
lifting its head through heavy Sunday sleep?

And later, going home, a moon rising
at the end of a cart-track, minimum of red,
the wind being dark, imperfect cows staring
out of their half-intelligence, and a plough
lying on its side in the cold, raw

naked twilight, there began to move
slowly, like heavy water, in the heart
the image of the gull and of that dress,
both being white and out of the darkness rising
the moon ahead of us with its rusty ring.

The chair in which you've sat

The chair in which you've sat is not just a chair
nor the table at which you've eaten just a table
nor the window that you've looked from just a window.
All these have now a patina of your
body and mind, a kind of ghostly glow
which haloes them a little, though invisible.

There is, said Plato, an ideal place
with immortal windows, tables and pure chairs,
archetypes of these, as yet unstained.
In such a world one might look out to space
and see pure roses yet untouched by hand,
the perfect patterns of a universe

of which our furniture is but editions
bred from a printing press which has no end.
The perfect Bible will remain unread
and what we have's a series of translations

which scholars make, each nodding aching head
bowed over texts they never can transcend,

and yet more lovely because truly human
as tables, chairs and windows in our world
are ours and loved because they taste of us.
Being who we are we must adore the common
copies of perfection, for the grace
of perfect things and angels is too cold.

So in this room I take the luminous
as being the halo of our sweat and love
which makes a chair more than a simple chair,
a table more than a table, dress than dress,
and startlingly striking out of the air
the tigerish access of a crumpled glove.

JOHN SMITH

Death at the Opera

Is this what death is like? I sit
Dressed elegantly in black and white, in an expensive
                                        seat,
Watching Violetta expire in Covent Garden.
How beautiful she is! As her voice lures me toward her
                                        death
The strings of the orchestra moisten my eyes with tears,
Though the tenor is too loud. Is this what death is like?
No one moves. Violetta coughs; stumbles toward the
                                        bed.
Twenty miles away in the country my father is dying.
Violetta catches at her throat. Let me repeat: My father
Is dying in a semi-detached house on a main road
Twenty miles off in the country. The skull is visible.

I do not want it to end. How exquisitely moving is
                                        death,
The approach to it. The lovers sob. Soon they will be
                                        wrenched apart.
How romantic it all is. Her hand is a white moth
Fluttering against the coverlet of the bed. The bones
Of my father's hands poke through his dry skin.
His eyes look into a vacancy of space. He spits into a
                                        cup.
In a few moments now Violetta will give up the ghost;
The doctor, the maid, the tenor who does not love her,
                                        will sob.
Almost, our hearts will stop beating. How refreshed we
                                        have been.
My father's clothes, too large for his shrunken frame,
Make him look like a parcel. Ah! The plush curtains are
                                        opening.

The applause! The applause! It drowns out the ugly
noise
Of my father's choking and spitting. The bright lights
Glitter far more than the 100-watt bulb at home.
Dear Violetta! How she enjoys the flowers, like wreaths,
Showered for her own death. She gathers them to her.
We have avoided the coffin. I think that my father
Would like a box of good plain beech, being a man
From Buckinghamshire, a man of the country, a man of
the soil.
I have seen my father, who is fond of animals, kill a cat
That was old and in pain with a blow from the edge of
his palm.
He buried it in the garden, but I cannot remember its
name.

Now the watchers are dispersing; the taxis drive away
Black in the black night. A huddle of people wait
Like mourners round the stage door. Is this what death
is like?
For Violetta died after all. It is merely a ghost,
The voice gone, the beautiful dress removed, who steps
in the rain.
Art, I conceive, is not so removed from life; for we look
at death
Whether real or imagined from an impossible distance
And somewhere a final curtain is always descending.
The critics are already phoning their obituaries to the
papers.
I do not think God is concerned with such trivial matters
But, father, though there will be no applause, die well.

JON STALLWORTHY

A Letter from Berlin

My dear,
          Today a letter from Berlin
where snow – the first of '38 – flew in,
settled and shrivelled on the lamp last night,
broke moth wings mobbing the window. Light
woke me early, but the trams were late:
I had to run from the Brandenburg Gate
skidding, groaning like a tram, and sodden
to the knees. Von Neumann operates at 10
and would do if the sky fell in. They lock
his theatre doors on the stroke of the clock –
but today I was lucky: found a gap
in the gallery next to a chap
I knew just as the doors were closing. Last,
as expected, on Von Showmann's list
the new vaginal hysterectomy
that brought me to Berlin.
                    Delicately
he went to work, making from right to left
a semi-circular incision. Deft
dissection of the fascia. The blood-
blossoming arteries nipped in the bud.
Speculum, scissors, clamps – the uterus
cleanly delivered, the pouch of Douglas
stripped to the rectum, and the cavity
closed. Never have I seen such masterly
technique. 'And so little bleeding!' I said
half to myself, half to my neighbour.
                    'Dead',
came his whisper. 'Don't be a fool'
I said, for still below us in the pool
of light the marvellous unhurried hands
were stitching, tying the double strands
of catgut, stitching, tying. It was like

a concert, watching those hands unlock
the music from their score. And at the end
one half expected him to turn and bend
stiffly towards us. Stiffly he walked out
and his audience shuffled after. But
finishing my notes in the gallery
I saw them uncover the patient: she
was dead.

> *I met my neighbour in the street*
waiting for the same tram, stamping his feet
on the pavement's broken snow, and said:
'I have to apologize. She was dead,
but how did you know?' Back came his voice
like a bullet '— saw it last month, twice'.

Returning your letter to an envelope
yellower by years than when you sealed it up,
darkly the omens emerge. A ritual wound
yellow at the lip yawns in my hand;
a turbulent crater; a trench, filled
not with snow only, east of Buchenwald.

A poem about Poems About Vietnam

The spotlights had you covered [*thunder*
in the wings]. In the combat zones
and in the Circle, darkness. Under
the muzzles of the microphones
you opened fire, and a phalanx
of loudspeakers shook on the wall;
but all your cartridges were blanks
when you were at the Albert Hall.

Lord George Byron cared for Greece,
Auden and Cornford cared for Spain,
confronted bullets and disease
to make their poems' meaning plain;
but you – by what right did you wear
suffering like a service medal,
numbing the nerve that they laid bare,
when you were at the Albert Hall?

The poets of another time –
Owen with a rifle-butt
between his paper and the slime,
Donne quitting Her pillow to cut
a quill – knew that in love and war
dispatches from the front are all.
We believe them, they were there,
when you were at the Albert Hall.

Poet, they whisper in their sleep
louder from underground than all
the mikes that hung upon your lips
when you were at the Albert Hall.

ANNE STEVENSON

A Daughter's Difficulties as a Wife: Mrs Reuben Chandler to her mother in New Orleans

September 3, 1840   Cincinnati, Ohio.

Now that I've been married for almost four weeks,
                                        Mama,
    I'd better drop you and Papa dear a line.
        I guess I'm fine.

Ruby has promised to take me to the Lexington
    buggy races Tuesday, if the weather cools.
        So far we've not been out much.

Just stayed here stifling in hot Cincinnati.
    Clothes almost melt me, Mama, so I've not got out
        my lovely red velvet-and-silk pelisse yet,

or that sweet little lambskin coat with the fur hood.
    The sheets look elegant!
        I adore the pink monogram on the turnover

with exactly the same pattern on the pillowcases!
    Darlings!
        How I wish you could breeze in and admire them!

And the table linen,
    and the bone china,
        and the grand silver candlesticks,

and especially those
    long-stemmed Venetian wine glasses
        with the silver rims.

226

My, didn't your little daughter
   play the queen the other day
      serving dinner to a whole bevy of bachelors!

To tell the truth, Mama,
   Reuben was a silly to ask them,
      just imagine me, tiny wee me,

hostess to fourteen dragons
   and famished monsters,
      doing battle with fuming pipes and flying plugs.

Poor Rube!
   He doesn't chew and hardly ever smokes.
      He must have felt out of place.

I was frantic, naturally,
   for fear of wine stains and
      tobacco juice on the table cloth,

so I set Agatha to dart in and dab with a towel,
   and told Sue in the kitchen, to brew up some coffee
      quick, before they began speechmaking.

But it was no use.
   They would put me up on a chair after the ices,
      and one of them – Big Tom they call him –

(runs a sizable drygoods business here)
   well, this Tom pulled off my shoe,
      tried to drink wine out of it while

I was dying of laughter,
   and Tom was laughing too, when suddenly
      I slipped, and fell on the Flemish decanter!

It broke.
   Such a terrible pity.
      And so funny at the same time.

I must admit the boys were bricks,
   carrying the tablecloth out to the kitchen,
      holding it out while I

poured hot water from a height,
   just as you always said to.
      Everything would have been all right.

The party could have gone on.
   Then Reuben had to nose in and spoil things,
      sending me to bed!

So the boys went off, kind of sheepish.

Later Reuben said I had disgraced us
   and where was I brought up anyway,
      to behave like a bar maid!

But it wasn't my fault, Mama.
   They were his friends. He invited them.
      I like to give men a good time!

I'm writing this in bed because
   my head thumps and drums every time I move
      and I'm so dog tired!

The only time I sleep is in the morning
   when Reuben has left for the office.
      Which brings up a *delicate* subject, Mama.

I've been thinking and thinking,
   wondering whether I'll *ever* succeed in being
      the tender, devoted little wife you wanted me to
                                             be.

Because . . . oh, Mama,
   why didn't you tell me or warn me before I was
                                        married
      that a wife is expected to do it *every night*!

But how could we have guessed?
  Ruby came courting so cool and fine and polite,
    while beneath that gentlemanly, educated
                                exterior . . .

well! I don't like to worry you, Mama.
  You know what men are like!
    I remember you said once the dears couldn't help
                                            it.

I try to be brave.
  But if you *did* have a chance to speak to Papa,
    mightn't you ask him to slip a word,

sort of man to man to Reuben . . .
  about how delicate I am
    and how sick I am every month,

not one of those cows
  who can be used and used?
    Someone's at the door.

I forgot,
  I asked Fanny Daniels to come up this morning
    to help fix a trim for my hat.

I'll have to hustle!
  Give all my love to dear Spooky and Cookie.
    How I miss them, the doggy darlings!

Oceans of hugs and kisses for you, too,
  and for precious Papa,

    From your suffering and loving daughter,

      Marianne

Willow Song
(for Frances Horowitz)

I went down to the railway
But the railway wasn't there.
A long scar lay across the waste
Bound up with vetch and maidenhair
And birdsfoot trefoils everywhere.
But the clover and the sweet hay,
The cranesbill and the yarrow
Were as nothing to the rose bay
    the rose bay, the rose bay,
As nothing to the rose bay willow.

I went down to the river
But the river wasn't there.
A hill of slag lay in its course
With pennycress and cocklebur
And thistles bristling with fur.
But ragweed, dock and bitter may
And hawkbit in the hollow
Were as nothing to the rose bay,
    the rose bay, the rose bay
As nothing to the rose bay willow.

I went down to find my love,
My sweet love wasn't there.
A shadow stole into her place
And spoiled the loosestrife of her hair
And counselled me to pick despair.
Old elder and young honesty
Turned ashen, but their sorrow
Was as nothing to the rose bay
    the rose bay, the rose bay,
As nothing to the rose bay willow.

O I remember summer
When the hemlock was in leaf.
The sudden poppies by the path
Were little pools of crimson grief,
Sick henbane cowered like a thief.
But self-heal sprang up in her way,
And mignonette's light yellow,
To flourish with the rose bay,
      the rose bay, the rose bay,
To flourish with the rose bay willow.

Its flames took all the wasteland
And all the river's silt,
But as my dear grew thin and grey
They turned as white as salt or milk.
Great purples withered out of guilt,
And bright weeds blew away
In cloudy wreathes of summer snow,
And the first one was the rose bay,
      the rose bay, the rose bay,
The first one was the rose bay willow.

Meeting, 1944
L.S. and M.S.

I opened the front door and stood
lost in admiration of
a girl holding a paper box,
and that is how I fell in love.

I've come, she said, *to bring you this,*
some work from the photographer –
or rather it's for a Miss D . . .
Would you pass it on to her?

She's my sister, but she's out.
You must wait for her inside.
I'm expecting her right now.
Come in. I held the front door wide.

We talked a little of the war.
of what I did and what she earned;
a few minutes it was, no more,
before my sister had returned.

You're going? Well, I'm off out too.
And so we rose from our two chairs.
I'll be back shortly, Lily dear.
Shall I see you down the stairs?

That's all there is. We met again
until they took the Jews away.
I won't be long. I'll see you soon.
Write often. What else could we say?

I think they were such simple times
we died among simplicities.
and all that chaos seemed to prove
was what a simple world it is

that lets in someone at the door
and sees a pair of lives go down
high hollow stairs into the rain
that's falling gently on the town.

R. S. THOMAS

Welsh History

We were a people taut for war; the hills
Were no harder, the thin grass
Clothed them more warmly than the coarse
Shirts our small bones.
We fought, and were always in retreat,
Like snow thawing upon the slopes
Of Mynydd Mawr; and yet the stranger
Never found our ultimate stand
In the thick woods, declaiming verse
To the sharp prompting of the harp.

Our kings died, or they were slain
By the old treachery at the ford.
Our bards perished, driven from the halls
Of nobles by the thorn and bramble.

We are a people bred on legends,
Warming our hands at the red past.
The great were ashamed of our loose rags
Clinging stubbornly to the proud tree
Of blood and birth; our lean bellies
And mud houses were a proof
Of our ineptitude for life.

We were a people wasting ourselves
In fruitless battles for our masters,
In lands to which we had no claim,
With men for whom we felt no hatred.

We were a people, and are so yet,
When we have finished quarrelling for crumbs
Under the table, or gnawing the bones
Of a dead culture, we will arise,
Armed, but not in the old way.

Welsh Landscape

To live in Wales is to be conscious
At dusk of the spilled blood
That went to the making of the wild sky,
Dyeing the immaculate rivers
In all their courses.
It is to be aware,
Above the noisy tractor
And hum of the machine
Of strife in the strung woods,
Vibrant with sped arrows.
You cannot live in the present,
At least not in Wales.
There is the language for instance,
The soft consonants
Strange to the ear.
There are cries in the dark at night
As owls answer the moon,
And thick ambush of shadows,
Hushed at the fields' corners.
There is no present in Wales,
And no future;
There is only the past,
Brittle with relics,
Wind-bitten towers and castles
With sham ghosts;
Mouldering quarries and mines;
And an impotent people,
Sick with inbreeding,
Worrying the carcase of an old song.

On the Farm

There was Dai Puw. He was no good.
They put him in the fields to dock swedes,
And took the knife from him, when he came home
At late evening with a grin
Like the slash of a knife on his face.

There was Llew Puw, and he was no good.
Every evening after the ploughing
With the big tractor he would sit in his chair,
And stare into the tangled fire garden,
Opening his slow lips like a snail.

There was Huw Puw, too. What shall I say?
I have heard him whistling in the hedges
On and on, as though winter
Would never again leave those fields,
And all the trees were deformed.

And lastly there was the girl:
Beauty under some spell of the beast.
Her pale face was the lantern
By which they read in life's dark book
The shrill sentence: God is love.

Threshold

I emerge from the mind's
cave into the worse darkness
outside, where things pass and
the Lord is in none of them.

I have heard the still, small voice
and it was that of the bacteria
demolishing my cosmos. I
have lingered too long on

this threshold, but where can I go?
To look back is to lose the soul
I was leading upward towards
the light. To look forward? Ah,

what balance is needed at
the edges of such an abyss.
I am alone on the surface
of a turning planet. What

to do but, like Michelangelo's
Adam, put my hand
out into unknown space,
hoping for the reciprocating touch?

ADAM THORPE

Neighbours

My mother noticed it first, that smell
the day before her yearly garden
barbecue; lemon soufflés
in the fridge, the wobble of trifle.
For days before she'd scanned the skies
as July wilted the dahlias, steamed
in the field left fallow behind.

The stench grew serious; by dusk
we had our fists to mouths, wondered
if the blue, rather beautiful ribbons
rippling in the thistles at the back
had anything to do with it.
We strolled to the wire of the garden,
saw through the draped convolvulus

the intimate colours of our neighbours
displayed on the field; the loud
ecstasy of flies above
what glittering clarity! – the tissue
scrolled amongst thistles, small gules
of cotton-wool, the fesse of the organic.
We stumbled back and my mother

spat, feeling her health go. Me
and my father trooped round in a column;
they yelled back about a blockage
in the septic tank, and brimming bowls.
It failed to rain, but the wind
veered somewhat, towards the wood.

When they came we told each not
to look beyond the wire. One
by one, in the middle of some bright
conversation, balancing their wine
on a plate of sausages and steak,
they'd glance, quickly, then turn their heads back,
the smile still frozen on their mouths.

ANTHONY THWAITE

The Bonfire

Day by day, day after day, we fed it
With straw, mown grass, shavings, shaken weeds,
The huge flat leaves of umbrella plants, old spoil
Left by the builders, combustible; yet it
Coughed fitfully at the touch of a match,
Flared briefly, spat flame through a few dry seeds
Like a chain of fireworks, then slumped back to the soil
Smouldering and smoky, leaving us to watch

Only a heavy grey mantle without fire.
This glum construction seemed choked at heart,
The coils of newspaper burrowed into its hulk
Led our small flames into the middle of nowhere,
Never touching its centre, sodden with rot.
Ritual petrol sprinklings wouldn't make it start
But swerved and vanished over its squat brown bulk,
Still heavily sullen, grimly determined not

To do away with itself. A whiff of smoke
Hung over it as over a volcano.
Until one night, late, when we heard outside
A crackling roar, and saw the far field look
Like a Gehenna claiming its due dead.
The beacon beckoned, fierily aglow
With days of waiting, hiding deep inside
Its bided time, ravenous to be fed.

Lesson

In the big stockyards, where pigs, cows, and sheep
Stumble towards the steady punch that beats
All sense out of a body with one blow,
Certain old beasts are trained to lead the rest
And where they go the young ones meekly go.

240

Week after week these veterans show the way,
Then, turned back just in time, are led themselves
Back to the pens where their initiates wait.
The young must cram all knowledge in one day,
But the old who lead live on and educate.

In the Gravel Pit

In the steady rain, in June,
In the gravel pit by the pylon,
This empty afternoon
Walking there in a dead
Mood, I found one
Not caught inside my head.
Caught quite otherwise,
What was a rabbit, just,
Crouched with its blank eyes
In a sodden lump of fur
In grey indeterminate mist.
It did not even stir
As I stood there in the rain.
Mud-trickles down the bank
Oozed under its paws. What pain
It felt I do not know.
The gravel pit had the stink
Of wet silage, of the slow
Decay of thrown-out stuff.
And as I stood and watched
This end of a scrap of life,
I did what I had to do.
For the first time, it twitched
As I stooped and set my hand to
A broken plank in the mud.
I struck maybe seven times,
Till its eyes burst, and its blood
Covered its wretched fur,
And no sound, no whimpers or screams,
Only my own roar

Of misery, ignorance, pain,
Alone in the gravel pit
By the pylon in the rain,
And my hand with its own blood
Torn by a nail that bit
As I struck at a dead mood
And an animal dying there
Without meaning in the mud
In the warm summer air,
With the rain still soaking the earth,
And everywhere, in the blood,
The dying, the giving birth.

CHARLES TOMLINSON

In the Studio

'Recorded ambience' – this
is what they call
silences put back
between the sounds:
leaves might fall
on to the roof-glass to compound
an instant ambience
from the drift of sibilants:
but winter boughs
cannot enter – they
distort like weed
under the glass water:
this (sifted) silence
now recording (one
minute only of it)
comprises what
you did not hear before
you began to listen –
the sighs that
in a giant building
rise up trapped between
its sound-proofed surfaces
murmuring, replying
to themselves, gathering
power like static
from the atmosphere: you do
hear this ambience?
it rings true: for silence
is an imagined thing.

Into Distance

Swift cloud
across still cloud
drifting east
so that the still
seems also on the move
the other way: a vast
opposition throughout the sky
and, as one stands
watching the separating
gauzes, greys, the eyes
wince dizzily away from them:
feeling for roots anew
one senses the strength
in planted legs, the pull
at neck, tilted
upwards to a blue that
ridding itself of all
its drift keeps now
only those few, still
islands clouds to occupy
its oceanic spread
where a single, glinting plane
bound on and over
is spinning into distance and ahead
of its own sound

The Journey

The sun had not gone down. The new moon
  Rose alongside us, set out as we did:
Grateful for this bright companionship
  We watched the blade grow sharp against the night
And disappear each time we dipped:
  A sliver of illumination at the crest
Awaited us, a swift interrogation
  Showed us the shapes we drove towards
And lost them to the intervening folds
  As our way descended. It was now
The travelling crescent suddenly began
  To leap from side to side, surprising us
At every fresh appearance, unpredictably
  Caught among the sticks of some right-hand tree
Or sailing left over roof and ridge
  To mock us. I know the explanation
But explanations are less compelling than
  These various returns and the expectancy that can
Never quite foresee the way
  The looked-for will look back at us
Across the deviousness of distances that keep on
  Lapsing and renewing themselves under a leaping
                                     moon.

JOHN TRIPP

Connection in Bridgend

In the bus café, drinking tea, I watch
nothing happening in Bridgend.
I mean, there is rain, some shoppers
under canopies, tyres sloshing them
from the gutters. Otherwise not much.

(Do those Pakistanis feel the cold?
What are they doing in Bridgend?
How did they land here, and those lost
Sikhs and Chinamen?
I am sorry for them, they look bereft.)

In the café a young mother is being given
stick by her two boys. They want Coke
and her baby cries for no reason
unless he's seen enough of Bridgend.
I feel an odd kinship with him.

At last my bacon sandwich is done;
it was something to look forward to,
slicing a minute's delight into the murk.
Balancing the plate, I hold the sad babe
while his mother fetches the Coke.

Then a one-armed paperseller comes in
with a strip of frayed ribbons on his coat.
He wants to tell me his story,
so I listen while the baby sobs
and his brothers suck straws.

An hour ago, I was alone; now
there are six. Even the café-owner
squeezes out a smile. We are in it

246

together, until the last buses go out.
One by one they leave the bays.

Ashes on the Cotswolds

He asked me to accompany him
to collect his sister-in-law's ashes
in Southampton, and then scatter them
somewhere on the Cotswolds.
She and her husband had honeymooned there.
His brother couldn't face it, he said.

It was a Saturday. We had to be there
before noon, when the place closed
(weren't people cremated on Saturdays?)
He owned a powerful Humber Hawk
and he drove like Fangio
to reach Southampton in time.

Was it the right urn? How
could we tell? We stopped for lunch
in Salisbury, and over the roast lamb he said:
'My sister-in-law's on the back seat of that car.'
Then we headed for the range
to keep his promise to his brother.

Somewhere near Cleeve Hill
he took the lid off the urn
and threw the ashes into the wind.
They blew back on us
as I tried to take a photograph
to send to his grieving brother.

The ashes disappeared on the wind
and were dust on our clothes.
We shook it off, and I took
a photo of the urn in the grass.
As we say on these occasions,
it was what she would have wanted.

GAEL TURNBULL

What Makes the Weeds Grow Tall

So tell me what we've done
to make the weeds grow tall.
          To make the weeds grow tall?
          It's just the rain and sun.
It's nothing else at all
as the earth spins on its track,
          always going coming back.
And Jack shall fancy Jill
          and Jill shall fancy Jack
until, until, until
          one day, Jack's tired of Jill.
Then alack, alack, alack
          if Jill's not tired of Jack
until she fancies Bill
          or maybe fancies Mac
who's always looking back
          and no one can keep track
for someone else again
          and then, and then, and then
and round and round it goes
          and no one really knows
          what makes the weeds grow tall
for no one knows at all
why Jack is after June
          (he'll tire of *her* quite soon)
or it might be Kate or Fran
          or Di or Sue or Ann.
So tell me what they've done
to deserve such endless fun
          as the earth spins on its course
for better and for worse
          till Jack shall find his Jill
(let's hope one day he will)
          and Jill shall find her Jack

(*and* be glad to have him back)
            after the sun has shone
and the rain has rained its fill.
            It's nothing we have done
            that makes the weeds grow tall
(to make the weeds grow tall!)
            and no one, no one, no one
            looks after them at all.

JOHN WAIN

Au Jardin des Plantes

The gorilla lay on his back,
One hand cupped under his head,
Like a man.

Like a labouring man tired with work,
A strong man with his strength burnt away
In the toil of earning a living.

Only of course he was not tired out with work,
Merely with boredom; his terrible strength
All burnt away by prodigal idleness.

A thousand days, and then a thousand days,
Idleness licked away his beautiful strength,
He having no need to earn a living.

It was all laid on, free of charge.
We maintained him, not for doing anything,
But for being what he was.

And so that Sunday morning he lay on his back,
Like a man, like a worn-out man,
One hand cupped under his terrible hard head.

Like a man, like a man,
One of those we maintain, not for doing anything,
But for being what they are.

A thousand days, and then a thousand days,
With everything laid on, free of charge,
They cup their heads in prodigal idleness.

Ode to a Nightingale

It's your sense of theatre, we realise, inconspicuous
drab brown communicator, that does it, your choice of
space and occasion to set off your performance:
that resplendent fame

didn't come to you in straight competition, for even
a cloth-eared amateur like me can discern that
in terms of pure aesthetics the thrush and the blackbird
in their ordinary urban

settings, back garden and chimney-pot, performing
at routine times when the sun is climbing or sinking,
make music that note for note need fear no comparison
with your artfullest descant;

what makes you a star is your *penchant* for shade and
                                                seclusion,
not mere dusk but the last hour of slow-motion nightfall
in June when the daylight has all but abolished the
                                                darkness,
yet part of that all-but

is the thrilling aria you launch unannounced from
                                        somewhere
one's eyes can seldom penetrate. Your love of the covert
adds that dimension of mystery all art needs; it's as well
not to parade your

act in the sunlight, for, besides the more bustling
competition, there is your totally unremarkable
appearance, the bird-world's equivalent of
our brief-cased commuters.

Our species could learn from you, except that we can't
learn from anything, being vain and unteachable.
We prod our artists into the spotlight, bring up
cameras and mikes

to record their banalities, place on embarrassing record
their threadbare opinions; like you, they're predictably
humdrum except when performing, but unlike you
they simply don't see it.

No, little brown bird, go on wisely ignoring
our foolish example; as you have been, continue:
from your shadowy perch, make the night grow reckless
                                        with music.
By your art we shall know you.

TED WALKER

New Forest Ponies

They stopped from a gallop. Steam
left them like epiphanies
loose in the dusk. I saw them
whisking at snowflakes like flies.

It was a pair of forest
mares, briskets slung like hammocks
of fat matelots. With rapt lust
they browsed remnants of picnics

beside the Brockenhurst road.
Hobos, they rifled litter-bins,
turfing out chicken bones; then stood
casually among beer-cans,

posed for a snapshot album.
I nudged them along the verge
until their stallion came
prancing a disremembered rage

through the ice twilight. His strength
was flagged, a softening thong
of wash-leather. The cushy south
where he lives, where I belong,

would paddock him for gymkhanas,
currying his fourteen hands
to a genteel handsomeness.
Now he smelt like failing ponds,

shut cinemas. He began to come
at me. Gripping the fence-post,
I waited. But he ambled, a tame
elderly man in tweeds, lost

in some reverie of war,
all wildness shrunk. White of eyes
was mush, the shown teeth sulphur
dull. He let me feel him – thews,

veins, worn cordage to the touch.
I held him grass on my palm.
He cadged himself a sandwich;
mooched away, slavering jam.

J. P. WARD

The Party

and finally the garden and
terrace were finished, and they
decided on a party, with salads, cheese,
and a bowl of strawberries, and Peter
and Sue came down the steps with a
bottle of wine and some mushrooms, and
others came, and they had a fat
trestle table, with dinner-plates with
cold meats on, ham, salami, chicken
and some pork, and on an old pub
table beside it, on the lawn edge,
were tomatoes cut into eighths, and
Jim and Hanna came next with their
unmarried aunt, and two or three
groups stood with a fork and paper
napkin in each hand, and a glass of
either red or rosé wine, or tomato
juice, and some had already entered
the cold apple pie, fruit from trees
on the wall, and there was potato
salad, celery, lettuce, and cress from
the stream, and some cold trout, smooth
on the tongue like butter, and all
the eaters stood, not sat, and Frank
was able to pick a rose-petal, and a
whole rose, waist-high, with oil-covered
fingers, where the terrace's slabs
met the lawn, and Shirley spoke to
Martin, handing him a slice of tongue,
and a cold mushroom salad was then
brought out, and shell-fish done with
larger cod in a cheese sauce, and a
child played on the terrace's slabs
with a wheel, looking like a radish

or two, and the apple pie's crust went
slowly up and down, and the juice made
it soggy, and cream licked it, and a
lean, dapper man pushed two sardines
with his fork, and with a cube of
bread in its oil, and Donald and Diana
came late, were uncertain but gave a
cask of ginger, and they finished some
uncut cucumber, tomatoes and lettuces,
and very crusty bread before the one
plum-pie as well as the three apple
pies, and by then the men were in
threes talking, the girls eating savoury
biscuits and cheese also with the men,
both in some cases, and the champagne
was in some cases, and George put his
plate of Camembert and Brie, and
strawberries, down on the terrace's
slabs for a minute, smiling to the
child to avoid it, and gave Jane some
more cream and red wine in a glass like
a tulip, and there were three red
tulips actually, at the slab's edge, and
I made this into a poem, for poetry is
a necessity, as is food.

The A40 Wolvercote Roundabout at Oxford

'O' the ubiquitous, the wheel.
A while if only for a while.
A lawn reflecting orange light.
A helipad whence to depart.

Why is he restless? Moons about,
Disturbs the static April night?
O the ubiquitous prayer-wheel,
The ring of lamp-posts tapering tall.

'Welcome to Scholars' Oxenford'
And watch the town roulette-wheel speed
Its bits of centrifugal thought
Off at all angles to the night

As cars brake to its edge, then yield
To let a prior group roar ahead
Then move themselves, or tucked behind
Swing to an exit out beyond,

An arc of concentrated thought.
He paced a little, sensed them do it,
Sat on a civic bench to watch
Them merge and hesitate, guess which

Split-second move a car would make
So miss some other overtake
Some other. None of them remained
More than an instant in his mind,

Not knowing what each driver bore
Most deeply, fears, obsessions, for
Those shed, like clothes, they dropped away
For one lone vagrant passer-by

Witnessing all their stop-start game.
He only saw them go and come
Lane-dodging, weaving, and the wheel
Their curvings made contain them all

As persons, work to suck them in
To this spun centre with its own
Illuminata, then away
'Stratford, The North', infinity.

ANDREW WATERMAN

In Memoriam Reggie Smith
(1914–1985)

It's like reaching to find no books on the shelf,
or turning with a smile to empty chair.
You trusted life as gift, gave of yourself.
Your postcard tells of projects in the air,
memoirs, a play, the Med. But the phone-call said
                                    you're dead.
How can I answer now when nothing's there?

'Pawn to King Four, old mate' . . . But I can't tip
the chess bits from the box to start again,
and hear that irksome ditty on your lip
as you cogitate, set traps, advance your men:
'By and by there'll be pie in the sky when you die.'
Plus, for you, booze, cricket, talk, sex, poets, pen.

Up there, there's very few you'd not let in:
sociologists? cheats? bosses? pedants? – you'll
still separate the sinner from the sin,
living, some carped, by sentimental rule.
'Is there no one Reggie hates?' 'Can't he discriminate?'
You brought our best out, and were no one's fool.

But I won't pretend you'd faith in any more
than human nature, though your own transcends
whatever is innate in any law
of physics . . . I've slipped gear to present tense,
a habit hard to kick – even after you got sick
you'd go anywhere for rugger, book-talk, friends.

Two strangers cast up on an island both
knew you, told your first novelizing wife.
From Wight to Perth to Dublin's Hill of Howth
we're all amputees still feeling you post-knife.

258

Farmers, writers, scientists; that Aussie tramp who
                              turned up pissed
in Derry: 'This fat Pom once saved my life.'

But your epicentre was the BBC.
Bliss was it in that dawn when radio
'Features' bet on creativity,
not output, ratings, costings, admin . . . So,
Dylan's *Milk Wood*, Louis's *Tower* – and 'The George'.
                              Until sour
compartmentalisers tidied up the show.

You kept that end up through the time you taught
our Coleraine students, scorning hacks who'd wall
poems behind analyses. You thought
teaching your 'privilege' – and taught us all.
As, decades back, meeting classes, helping victims, till
                              the Nazis
chased you from the Balkans at their fall.

Remember King's Cross? – scrambling to miss
a train, we sought the bar. Pints on our knees,
'The moon shines bright. In such a night as this,'
you quoted, 'wind did gently kiss the trees . . .
Let the sound of music creep in our ears . . .' You took
                              a deep
draught, 'Sheer magic, everyone agrees;

but what time-serving academic guff
ignores is – why on earth did Shakespeare pick,
from the play's couples, them for lyric stuff? –
him a ponce and scrounger up to any trick,
her a traitor to her Dad and culture, thief, a bad
lot – delinquents both, ripe for the nick.

So what was going on in Shakespeare's head?
Had he forgotten they were shits? Or just,
wanting some uplift to send folk to bed,
didn't care? No, rather, you can trust

that, attuned to what is real, he knew even shits can
                                                                    feel
in such a night there's more to it than lust.'

I glance out. Crewe. 5am. Right I write
you, mover, on the move; and to my kid;
the boat, this sleeper. You backed my doomed fight
(that drivelling judge) for custody, amid
your illness and tax-hash. Your card ends, 'Soon more
                                                                    cash
to help.' Reg, I owe you five hundred quid.

From your start spark-bright in dour depression Brum –
you'd all its ballads; and the Afghan Wars' –
you never lost, however far you'd come,
an axial sense of truth and a just cause.
The world's a smaller place, that can't look up and see
                                                                    your face.
Last week Earth missed a heartbeat: it was yours.

HUGO WILLIAMS

Walking Out of the Room Backwards

Out of work at fifty, smoking fifty a day,
my father wore his sheepskin coat
and went to auditions
for the first time in his life.
I watched in horror from my bedroom window
as he missed the bus to London
in full view of the house opposite.
'If it weren't for you and the children,'
he told my mother from his bed,
'I'd never get up in the morning.'

He wasn't amused
when I burst in on his sleep
with a head hollowed out of a turnip
swinging from a broom. There were cigarette burns
like bullet-holes in his pyjamas.
I saw his bad foot
sticking out from under the bedclothes
because he was 'broke'
and I thought my father was dying.
I wanted to make him laugh, but I got it wrong
and only frightened myself.

The future stands behind us, holding ready
a chloroform-soaked handkerchief.
The past stretches ahead, into which we stare,
as into the eyes of our parents
on their wedding day –
shouting something from the crowd
or waving things on sticks
to make them look at us. To punish me,
or amuse his theatrical friends,
my father made me walk out of the room backwards,
bowing and saying, 'Goodnight, my liege.'

DAVID WRIGHT

A Funeral Oration

Composed at thirty, my funeral oration: here lies
David John Murray Wright, 6′ 2″, myopic blue eyes;
Hair grey (very distinguished looking, so I am told);
Shabbily dressed as a rule; susceptible to cold;
Acquainted with what are known as the normal vices;
Perpetually short of cash; useless in a crisis;
Preferring cats, hated dogs; drank (when he could) too
                                        much;
Was deaf as a tombstone; and extremely hard to touch.
Academic achievements: B.A., Oxon (2nd class);
Poetic: the publication of one volume of verse,
Which in his thirtieth year attained him no fame at all
Except among intractable poets, and a small
Lunatic fringe congregating in Soho pubs.
He could roll himself cigarettes from discarded stubs,
Assume the first position of Yoga; sail, row, swim;
And though deaf, in church appear to be joining a
                                        hymn.
Often arrested for being without a permit,
Starved on his talents as much as he dined on his wit,
Born in a dominion to which he hoped not to go back
Since predisposed to imagine white possibly black:
His life, like his times, was appalling; his conduct odd;
He hoped to write one good line; died believing in God.

Monologue of a Deaf Man

> *Et lui comprit trop bien, n'ayant pas entendu.*
> Tristan Corbière

It is a good plan, and began with childhood
As my fortune discovered, only to hear
How much it is necessary to have said. ·

262

Oh silence, independent of a stopped ear,
You observe birds, flying, sing with wings instead.

Then do you console yourself? You are consoled
If you are, as all are. So easy a youth
Still unconcerned with the concern of a world
Where, masked and legible, a moment of truth
Manifests what, gagged, a tongue should have told;

Still observer of vanity and courage
And of these mirror as well; that is something
More than a sound of violin to assuage
What the human being most dies of: boredom
Which makes hedgebirds clamour in their blackthorn
                                                cage.

But did the brushless fox die of eloquence?
No, but talked himself, it seems, into a tale.
The injury, dominated, is an asset;
It is there for domination, that is all.
Else what must faith do deserted by mountains?

Talk to me then, you who have so much to say,
Spectator of the human conversation,
Reader of tongues, examiner of the eye,
And detective of clues in every action,
What could a voice, if you heard it, signify?

The tone speaks less than a twitch and a grimace.
People make to depart, do not say 'Goodbye'.
Decision, indecision, drawn on every face
As if they spoke. But what do they really say?
You are not spared, either, the banalities.

In whatever condition, whole, blind, dumb,
One-legged or leprous, the human being is,
I affirm the human condition is the same,
The heart half broken in ashes and in lies,
But sustained by the immensity of the divine.

263

Thus I too must praise out of a quiet ear
The great creation to which I owe I am
My grief and my love. O hear me if I cry
Among the din of birds deaf to their acclaim
Involved like them in the not unhearing air.

By the Effigy of St Cecilia

Having peculiar reverence for this creature
Of the numinous imagination, I am come
To visit her church and stand before the altar
Where her image, hewn in pathetic stone,
Exhibits the handiwork of her executioner.

There are the axemarks. Outside, in the courtyard,
In shabby habit, an Italian nun
Came up and spoke: I had to answer, 'Sordo.'
She said she was a teacher of deaf children
And had experience of my disorder.

And I have had experience of her order,
Interpenetrating chords and marshalled sound;
Often I loved to listen to the organ's
Harmonious and concordant interpretation
Of what is due from us to the creation.

But it was taken from me in my childhood
And those graduated pipes turned into stone.
Now, having travelled a long way through silence,
Within the church in Trastevere I stand
A pilgrim to the patron saint of music

And am abashed by the presence of this nun
Beside the embodiment of that legendary
Virgin whose music and whose martyrdom
Is special to this place: by her reality.
She is a reminder of practical kindness,

264

The care it takes to draw speech from the dumb
Or pierce with sense the carapace of deafness;
And so, of the plain humility of the ethos
That constructed, also, this elaborate room
To pray for bread in; they are not contradictory.

Encounter

At Lisbon, in the Jardim Zoologico,
By the dilapidated palace where I loiter
This light and shady afternoon of October
Admiring deer, and pools, and azulejo'd

Fountains and cages – the various and quiet
Visible world, whether animate or made –
All things seem extraordinary and placid.
Fronds of jacaranda, transparent as feathers

Where seals, delighted, splash in their pond! Flamingos
Barely move, and then with the intensest grace.
There are the gazelles and Siberian tigers,
But no less strange or beautiful than these

A woman with children, like a composite flower
With children for petals. They hold her skirt and each
                                        other,
Hand in blind hand, linked figures of a frieze.
And neither they nor I admit misfortune.

They disappear, hand in hand, down the avenues
Enjoying the feel of the wind, of the sun and shadows,
And listening, as I do not, to the queer and sweet cries
Of the birds and odd beasts gathered in the garden.

Every Day in Every Way

(Dr. Coué: Every day in every way I grow better and better)

When I got up this morning
I thought the whole thing through:
Thought, Who's the hero, the man of the day?
Christopher, it's you.

With my left arm I raised my right arm
High above my head:
Said, Christopher, you're the greatest.
Then I went back to bed.

I wrapped my arms around me,
No use counting sheep.
I counted legions of myself
Walking on the deep.

The sun blazed on the miracle,
The blue ocean smiled:
We like the way you operate,
Frankly, we like your style.

Dreamed I was in a meadow,
Angels singing hymns,
Fighting the nymphs and shepherds
Off my holy limbs.

A girl leaned out with an apple,
Said, You can taste for free.
I never touch the stuff, dear,
I'm keeping myself for me.

Dreamed I was in heaven,
God said, Over to you,

Christopher, your're the greatest!
And Oh, it's true, it's true!

I like my face in the mirror,
I like my voice when I sing.
My girl says it's just infatuation –
I know it's the real thing.

Personal Advertisement

TASTY GEEZER/STUCK IN SNEEZER/YEAR BEFORE/GETS
                                        OUT/
SEEKS/SLOW-WITTED/GIANT-TITTED/SOCIOLOGIST
                                    VISITOR/
WHO LIKES/TO MESS ABOUT/

BLOKE NEEDS POKE/SEND PICS/BOX 6/

MASON/COUNCILLOR/MAGISTRATE/SOMETIME/
                        CONSERVATIVE/
CANDIDATE/JOGGER/SQUASH-PLAYER/FIRST-CLASS SHAPE/
SEEKS SIMILAR/VIEW RAPE/

BLOKE NEEDS POKE/SEND PICS/BOX 6/

SAD DOG/SEEKS TAIL/OLD BEAST/GROWN FRAIL/SNIFFING/
WORLD/FEELS MORE THAN/BITOUTOF/HELL WITH
                        THAT/HUNTS/
OLDER CAT/TO MEET/GRAB/BEAT THE/SHITOUTOF/

BLOKE NEEDS POKE/SEND PICS/BOX 6/

WHAT/THE WINTER/NEEDS/IS STARLIGHT/WHAT/THE
                        BLIND MAN/
NEEDS/IS LUCK/WHAT DIS BOY/NEED IS A/WEEK IN DE/SACK/
WIN WUNNADEM/REAL/BIGASS SISTERS/DAT/COMES/LIKE
                        A TRUCK/

BLOKE NEEDS POKE/SEND PICS/BOX 6/

LONG-FACED/LANKY/EVANGELICAL/WIFE EVANGELICAL/
INTEREST/
SANKEY/MOTHER-IN-LAW/EVANGELICAL/CRANKY/SEEKS
ANYBODY/
VIEW/HANKY-PANKY/

BLOKE NEEDS POKE/SEND PICS/BOX 6/

PRIME MINISTER/FANCYING/CHANGE OF PACE/PLANS
SPOT OF/
NONSENSE/BACK AT HER PLACE/ON REGULAR BASIS/NO
AIRS/
GRACES/WOMEN OR MEN/POP IN/FOR A NAUGHTY/AT NO
TEN/

ONE PART/IRISH/THREE PARTS/PISSED/SIX FOOT/SEVEN
AND/
NEVER BEEN/KISSED/WHERE/ARE YOU/

BLOKE NEEDS POKE/BOX 6/
FORGET ABOUT THE PICS

Elizabeth

(In the summer of 1968 thousands of people turned out at the
small stations along the route to see the train carrying the
body of Robert Kennedy from New York to Arlington
Memorial Cemetery in Washington. In Elizabeth, New Jersey,
three people were pressed forward on to the line by the crowd
and killed by a train coming the other way – I happened to
be travelling up by the next train in this direction and passed
the bodies. One was of a black woman.)

Up from Philadelphia,
Kennedy on my mind,
Found you waiting in Elizabeth,
Lying there by the line.

Up from Philadelphia,
Wasn't going back,
Saw you, then saw your handbag
Forty yards on up the track.

Saw you under a blanket,
Black legs sticking through,
Thought a lot about Kennedy,
Thought a lot about you.

Years later,

Blood on the line, blood on the line,
Elizabeth,
No end, no end to anything,
Nor any end to death.

No public grief by television,
Weeping all over town,
Nobody locked the train up
That struck the mourners down.

Nobody came to see you,
You weren't lying in state.
They swept you into a siding
And said the trains would be late.

They left you there in the siding
Against an outhouse wall
And the democratic primaries,
Oh they weren't affected at all,

In no way,

Blood on the line, blood on the line,
Elizabeth,
No end, no end to anything,
Nor any end to death.

Sirhan shot down Kennedy,
A bullet in L.A.,
But the one that broke Elizabeth,
It was coming the other way,

Coming on out of nowhere,
Into nowhere sped,
Blind as time, my darling,
Blind nothing in its head.

Elizabeth, Oh Elizabeth,
I cry your name and place
But you can't see under a blanket,
You can't see anyone's face,

Crying

Blood on the line, blood on the line,
Elizabeth,
No end, no end to anything,
Nor any end to death.

270

ACKNOWLEDGEMENTS

Fleur Adcock for 'Leaving the Tate'.

Allison and Busby for 'Fifteen Million Bags' from *For Beauty Douglas* by Adrian Mitchell.

Anvil Press for 'Standing Female Nude' from *Standing Female Nude* by Carol Ann Duffy; for 'The Virgin Punishing the Infant' by Carol Ann Duffy from *Selling Manhattan*; for 'Mending the Fire' and 'On the Brink of the Pit' by David Holbrook, from *Selected Poems*.

Canongate for 'The Piano Tuner' from *Each Bright Eye* by Valerie Gillies; for 'Invitation' from *Rough Seas* by Tom Pow.

Curtis Brown for 'The Bonfire', 'Lesson' and 'In the Gravel Pit' from *Poems 1953–1988* by Anthony Thwaite (published by Hutchinson).

The Estate of Thomas Blackburn for 'Francis Bacon', from *Post Mortem*, published by Rondo Publications.

Bloodaxe for 'Disturbance' from *Night Cries* by John Cassidy; for 'Watching for Dolphins' from *Watching for Dolphins* by David Constantine.

George Mackay Brown for 'Ikey on the People of Hellya' and 'Love Letter'.

Michael Burn for 'In Japan' from *Open Day and Night*.

Carcanet New Press for 'The Faithful Wife' and 'The Letter' from *Collected Poems* by Patricia Beer; for 'Gallop' from *Dreams of Power* by Alison Brackenbury; for 'The Hare' and 'Overheard in County Sligo' from *Selected Poems* by Gillian Clarke; for 'Cherry Ripe', 'The Fountain' and 'Put Not Your Trust in Princes' from *Collected Poems* and *To Scorch or Freeze* by Donald Davie; for 'Stopping Places' by Molly Holden from *Selected Poems*; for 'Strawberries' and 'The First Men on Mercury' from *Selected Poems* by Edwin Morgan; for 'An Allusion to Propertius' and 'The Herb Garden' from *Collected Poems* by C H Sisson; for 'Old Women', 'Two Girls Singing' and 'By Ferry to the Island' from *Selected Poems* by Iain Crichton Smith; for 'In Memorian Reggie Smith' from *Selected Poems* by Andrew Waterman.

Chatto and Windus for 'Daughter' from *The Grey Among the Green* by John Fuller; for 'On Sizewell Beach' from *The Ballad of the Yorkshire Ripper* by Blake Morrison; for 'Bro' and the section from 'This is Your Subject Speaking' from *Natural Causes* by Andrew Motion; for 'Seroyeshky' from *Selected Poems* by Carol Rumens; for 'A Letter from Berlin' and 'A Poem about Poems about Poems about Vietnam' from *The Anzac Sonata* by Jon Stallworthy.

Andre Deutsch for 'Merlin' from *For the Unfallen*, for 'Funeral Music 3 and 7' from *King Log* and 'Idylls of the King' from *Tenebrae* by Geoffrey Hill.

Faber for 'Engineers' Corner' from *Making Cocoa for Kingsley Amis* by Wendy Cope; for 'The Patricians', 'The Friendship of Young Poets', 'Leaving Dundee' and 'A Snow-Walk' from *Terry Street*, *The Happier Life*, *Elegies*, and *Northlight* by Douglas Dunn; for 'Son and Heir' and 'From the Fast Train' from *Cat's Whisker* by Philip Gross; for 'Vox Humana', 'From the Wave', 'Yoko' and 'Hide and Seek' from *Selected Poems* and *The Passages of Joy* by Thom Gunn; for 'The Outlaw', 'The Skunk', 'Punishment' and a section of 'Clearances' from *Selected Poems*, *North* and *The Haw Lantern* by Seamus Heaney; for 'Ancient Evenings' from *Acrimony* by Michael Hofmann, for 'Witches', 'Thrushes', 'How Water Began to Play' and 'Roe Deer' from *Collected Poems* by Ted Hughes; for 'The Whitsun Weddings' and 'Sad Steps' from *The Whitsun Weddings* and *High Windows* by Philip Larkin; for 'Cuba' and 'Why Brownlee Left' from *Selected Poems* by Paul Muldoon; for 'Second-Rate Republics' and 'Pot Burial' from *The Strange Museum* by Tom Paulin; for 'A Tune' from *Katerina Brac* by Christopher Reid; for 'Thaw' from *The Player Queen's Wife* by Oliver Reynolds.

Gomer Press for 'A Storm in Childhood' from *Collected Poems* by T H Jones.

Grafton for 'Welsh Landscape' and 'On the Farm' from *Song at the Year's Turning* and *The Bread of Truth* by R S Thomas.

David Higham Associates Ltd for 'Ou Frontis', 'Timothy Winters' and 'Family Feeling' from *Collected Poems* and *A*

272

Field of Vision by Charles Causley (published by Macmillan); for 'Song at the Beginning of Autumn', 'In the Night' and 'Euthanasia' from *Selected Poems* and 'Moments of Grace' by Elizabeth Jennings; for 'On the Patio' and 'Orchard with Wasps' by Peter Redgrove from *The Moon Dispenses*.

Michael Hamburger 'A Poet's Progress' and 'Solidarity' from *Ownerless Earth*.

Tony Harrison for 'Them and Uz', 'Book Ends' and 'Long Distance 2' from *Continuous*.

Hutchinson for 'Teaching Wordsworth' and 'Laudanum' from *Selected Poems* by Thomas Blackburn; for 'Office Party', 'Formosavej' and 'In a Restaurant' from *Collected Poems* by Alan Brownjohn; for 'An Attitude of Mind' and 'Frozen Canal' from *Attitude of Mind* by John Cassidy; for 'Visiting Hour' and 'Farm Funeral' from *Under the Ice* and *An Ear to the Ground* by Stewart Conn; for 'Animal Tamer' and 'Introspection of a Sibyl' from *Selected Poems* by Ruth Fainlight; for 'Anniversary' and 'Mother Love' from *Some Unease and Angels* by Elaine Feinstein; for 'Ode to a Nightingale' from *Open Country* by John Wain; for 'Everyday in Every Way', 'Personal Advertisement' and 'Elizabeth' from *Poems 1974–1983* by Kit Wright.

James Kirkup for 'No More Hiroshimas' and 'Waiting for the Train to Start'.

Liz Lochhead for 'Revelation' and 'Song of Solomon'.

Alastair Maclean for 'Rams', 'In Time of Breaking of Nations', 'Question and Answer' and 'Cloud Shout'.

Derek Mahon for 'Achill' from the *Poetry Book Society Anthology 1986/1987* published by Hutchinson.

Gerda Mayer for 'Lucky' from *Monkey on the Analyst's Couch*.

The Marvell Press for 'Church Going' and 'At Grass' from *The Less Deceived* by Philip Larkin.

Robert Minhinnick for 'Short Wave' and 'Sunday Morning'.

New Beacon Books for 'Lucy's Letter' from *Lucy's Letters and Loving* by James Berry.

Oxford University Press for 'For a Five Year Old', 'Future

273

Work' and 'The Bullaun' from *Selected Poems* by Fleur Adcock; for 'Jingle Bells', 'Master Kung at the Keyboard', 'Seaside Sensation' and 'Abbey Going' from *Collected Poems* by D J Enright; for 'Toyland' and 'Paraphrases' and 'A Sign Illuminated' from *Collected Poems* by Roy Fisher; for 'The Return' and 'The Snow Party' from *Poems 1962–1978* by Derek Mahon; for 'To the Nightingale' from *Venus and the Rain* by Medbh McGuckian; for one of the poems from 'Three Poems for Music', 'Mort aux Chats', 'An Exequy' and 'Non Piangere Liu' from *Collected Poems* by Peter Porter; for 'Behaviour of Dogs', 'Flying to Belfast, 1977' and 'A Martian Sends a Postcard Home' from *The Onion, Memory* by Craig Raine; for 'Big Ideas with Loose Connections' from *Arcadia* by Christopher Reid; for 'Broken Moon' and 'Mouthfuls' from *Broken Moon* by Carole Satyamurti; for 'A Daughter's Difficulties as a Wife' and 'Willow Song' from *Selected Poems 56–86* by Anne Stevenson; for 'In the Studio', 'Into distance', and 'The Journey' from *Collected Poems* by Charles Tomlinson; for 'Walking out of the Room Backwards' from *Writing Home* by Hugo Williams.

Penguin Books for 'In a Notebook' from *The Memory of War* by James Fenton; for 'Wounds' from *Poems 1963–1983* by Michael Longley.

Peterloo for 'Not My Best Side', 'Rising Damp' and 'Soothing and Awful' from *Selected Poems* by U A Fanthorpe; for 'Sir Brooke Boothby' and 'Make Believe' from *A Heartache of Grass* by Gerda Mayer.

Peters, Fraser and Dunlop for 'Prayer to Saint Grobianus' from *Melting into the Foreground* by Roger McGough.

Poetry Wales Press (Seren Books) for 'Elegy for the Welsh Dead in the Falkland Islands' from *Blodeuwedd* by Tony Conran; for 'The Freezer' and 'Summer in Greece' from *Selected Poems* and *The Last Candles* by Tony Curtis; for 'My Grandfather and the Apple Tree', 'The Key', and 'Cathedral Builders' from *Selected Poems* by John Ormond; for 'A Glass Window' and 'Lear at Fifty' from *Selected Poems* by Leslie Norris; for 'Do You Think We'll Ever Get to See Earth' from *Earth Studies and Other Voyages* by

Sheenagh Pugh; for 'Ashes on the Cotswolds' and 'Connection in Bridgend' from *Collected Poems* by John Tripp; for 'The Party' from *To Get Clear* and 'The A40 Wolvercote Roundabout to Oxford' by J P Ward.

Sheenagh Pugh for 'Frozen Field'.

Alastair Reid for 'The O-Filler' from *Weathering* published by Canongate.

Peter Redgrove for 'Entry'.

Robson Books for 'Taken in Adultery', 'No Sense of Direction', 'I'm Covered Now' and 'Collected Poems Recollected' from *Collected Poems* and *Funeral Games* by Vernon Scannell; for 'Death at the Opera' from *Selected Poems* by John Smith.

Rogers, Coleridge and White for *Dusk, Burnham-Overy-Straithe* from *The Rain Giver* by Kevin Crossley-Holland.

Alan Ross for 'Stanley Matthews' from *Collected Poems*.

Routledge and Kegan Paul for 'Death of a Son' and 'Daisy' from *Selected Poems* by Jon Silkin.

Secker and Warburg for 'Song of a Battery Hen' by Edwin Brock; for 'Double Bass' and 'Valentine' from *Collected Poems* by John Fuller; for 'Bridal' from *A Jump Start* by James Lasdun; for 'A Scarecrow' from *In the Hall of the Saurians* by Peter Redgrove; for 'Neighbours' from *Mornings in the Baltic* by Adam Thorpe.

Anthony Sheil Associates for 'Poem for Breathing', 'In Love with Red' and 'A Field of Rape' by George MacBeth.

James Simmons for 'Claudy' from *Collected Poems*.

The estate of John Tripp for 'Connection in Bridgend' and 'Ashes on the Cotswolds'.

Ted Walker for 'New Forest Ponies'.

George Szirtes for 'Meeting, 1944'.

R S Thomas for 'Welsh History' and 'Threshold' from *Between Here and Now*.

Gael Turnbull for *What Makes the Weeds Grow Tall?*